The Tale of Two Churches

The Tale of Two Churches

William Floyd Dopp

This book is dedicated to faithful Christians
everywhere and especially to my wife Janet and
our family. God's love is our common bond.

Order this book online at www.trafford.com
or email orders@trafford.com

Most Trafford titles are also available at major online book retailers.

Printed in Victoria, BC, Canada.

ISBN: 978-1-4269-1785-1 (sc)
ISBN: 978-1-4269-1786-8 (hc)

Library of Congress Control Number: 2009939959

*Our mission is to efficiently provide the world's finest, most comprehensive book publishing
service, enabling every author to experience success. To find out how to publish your
book, your way, and have it available worldwide, visit us online at www.trafford.com*

Trafford rev. 12/04/2009

 www.trafford.com

North America & international
toll-free: 1 888 232 4444 (USA & Canada)
phone: 250 383 6864 ♦ fax: 812 355 4082

CONTENTS

INTRODUCTION:
The Two Churches of Our Times

As I began to prepare this book, one of my parishioners asked me, "What is its title?" Since I didn't have anything in mind at that time, I could only answer that I was writing about the two systematic types of churches in the Christian faith today. After looking at me with a blank stare he said, "Why not just call it the tale of two churches?" The title has stuck in my mind, so with thanks to that fine man, here is *The Tale of Two Churches*.

In these pages I will offer experiences of churches and individuals who are being transformed into something new. The examples are evidence of a new mission of the universal (holy catholic) church. The examples offered here are true, but some of the names have been changed or omitted to protect privacy. Also, my opinions are based on my experience and are not offered to change anyone's mind, but rather to encourage honest debate among faithful Christians. My purpose is to stimulate thought about the emergence of a new missionary movement to which the church is being called.

The two churches offered in these pages are not defined by denomination or even by theology. They are not defined by style of worship. These things represent the diversity of the holy catholic church, not the two churches I intend to discuss. There are many styles of congregations included in each of the two churches that I call the churches of our times.

At first glance, these days, one could make a good argument that the two predominant churches are *born-again evangelical* and *socially liberal*. The so-called Christian right and the progressive liberal churches are the ones making all the headlines. The truth is that most people in our churches today do not fall into either of these two camps. In the 2008 U.S. elections, for example, young, supposedly conservative evangelicals voted for many liberal candidates and supported some traditionally liberal issues. On the other hand, older members of what are considered liberal churches voted for conservative candidates. Of course, there are exceptions, and that is the point. There are individuals who are social conservatives and fiscal liberals, and vice versa. The polar extremes of these two groups get all the press, but in fact the people are not divided by clear lines. They do not define the two types of churches I will offer here.

When I refer to liberals and conservatives in the church I am speaking of the standard understanding of the use of those terms in society today. Those in the pews of mainline Protestant churches are more conservative than liberal, but most clergy are somewhat liberal. Congregational research in several 2008 denominational studies shows that the clergy, particularly in mainline churches, are more liberal than their people. Even among evangelical clergy there is a growing liberalism, particularly in support of human rights. One ecumenical study group I attended came to the conclusion that what divides conservatives and liberals in the church these days is the altar rail. For decades liberal leaders of most denominations have been choosing liberal candidates for ordination and then educating them at mostly liberal seminaries.

Meanwhile, it has been my experience that the person in the pew is asking the question, what has happened to my church?

While all of this has been going on, no one seems to be watching the store. Liberal political and social issues have taken the church's attention. The issues of the church's mission, particularly evangelism and outreach, are often going unattended. As for the people, they just want to be faithful and pray to God. Often they feel abandoned by the church they once knew and are searching for something new.

The two churches that I will explore are defined by the way they live out the Christian faith. They represent two distinct systems within the context of many styles. One church is self-centered, the other is Christ-centered. Survival is the concern of the self-centered, mission and ministry is the calling of the Christ-centered. The systemic differences are centered on the way people relate to each other in mission, how they understand the faith, and how they reach out beyond their own doors.

There are liberals and conservatives in both types of congregations. These two churches both have good and faithful Christians as members, but the latter has a mission. I call them the *old chapel church* (OCC) and the *emerging missionary church* (EMC). The old chapel church is the place where an individual prays; the emerging missionary church is the place where people pray together, and then go out into the world to do the work of the Body of Christ. People come to a chapel and go out from a mission. In these pages we will explore how this works.

I refer to the missionary church as emerging because it is a work in progress. It is in the process of finding its way to where God wants it to be. Of course, the church is always evolving as it is led by the Holy Spirit to do God's will. The EMC is the new church of our times. It has similarities to mission churches throughout history, but today's version is being called to face challenges never known before. It is emerging to bring godly order to the secular chaos in our rapidly changing world. Things like multicultural societies, interdependent world economics, instant global communications, and ethnic and tribal hatred are things the OCC never knew.

The OCC in History

For most of the two thousand years of church history, the OCC has served well enough. From the year 314 when Constantine was converted and made the Christian faith legal in the Roman Empire, until the end of World War II when national borders began to change dramatically, people worshiped at what was the OCC, the church of their nationality. For most of that time the OCC was Christ-centered. It was not until changes in society forced it into a survival mode that the OCC became self-centered.

These chapel churches were led into mission from time to time. The Great Reformation had many marks of mission and so did the missionary movements of the 1800s.

Before the Reformation, all in the western church were Roman Catholic after the 1517 reforms, and until just recently, most people identified with their nationality. Scandinavians and Germans were Lutheran, Brits were Anglicans, even in the many places where they dragged their empire, Italians and Irish were Catholic, Greeks were Orthodox, and later Americans honored nationality and were basically Protestant. Still later, Russians became Communists, but in time we would see that their Orthodox faith remained in their hearts. All of these churches were OCC.

Since the fall of Communism in the late 1980s and the advent of instant global communications, the world has become what is popularly called a *global village*. The nationality-driven OCC congregations may still exist, but they are not called to serve only their own. Many of them are finding their way to the EMC.

An Orthodox church near my home has ended its Greek services because very few of their people speak the language. An Irish friend of mine who married a Russian girl is now attending this Greek Orthodox Church. Who would have thought?

The EMC in Our Diverse World

What has developed is a need for diverse ministry. It is only the EMC that can minister to the diversity of people and their needs in today's complex multicultural world. People in all parts of the world seek God's peace and justice. Especially in some parts of the world where Islamic fundamentalism and ethnic hatred have raised their ugly heads, the OCC is powerless to offer peace or justice. It has little influence outside of its own sphere. On the other hand, the mission church offers hope. The EMC may not always convert people of other religions, but through its diverse makeup it can offer an example of love and care. That can be a very positive step toward world peace and justice.

As the chapels have failed, new missionaries are being called to renew the faith of a world seeking hope. It is the EMC that will emerge, sending its people out in the world for this task.

I admit that I am motivated by the EMC. I like to consider myself a missionary. I have witnessed mission churches and the power of the Holy Spirit coming from them in places where I have ministered. I saw energy among people in California where I served as a mission vicar, later as a canon missioner, and still later as archdeacon and assistant to the bishop. I discovered what a large number of very diverse people there were in mission.

I also witnessed mission among the good people of St. Martin's Episcopal Church in Hudson, Florida, where I served as their rector and pastor. Also, in the Diocese of Southwest Florida I have been blessed to be part of a variety of mission activity among a group of leaders engaged in outreach. In both California and Florida I have witnessed the church emerging in new missions. I have seen people come together to create wonderful ministries, things that none of them could have done on their own.

In EMC congregations I have consulted with throughout the United States and Canada, I have seen growth, and I have seen them prosper in newly developing areas as people were led to Christ. I have had the privilege of helping start new mission-based congregations that have brought the faith to thousands.

My most recent experience has been in Florida. I came to love the wonderful group of devoted disciples at St. Martin's. Like EMC congregations everywhere, these faithful people are true missionaries in their own community. They serve more than twenty local agencies from Hospice to the homeless. The parish has nearly thirty active ministries with almost seventy percent of the people involved in one or more of these efforts. These good folks know what it is to be the Body of Christ. Enthusiasm, one could feel it at St. Martin's. As one woman put it after one of our events, "What we did was like electricity, you could feel it."

Their hands and feet are the living God, walking and working among the people of their community. In my time at St. Martin's I saw the congregation grow as it expanded its ministries. The parish growth was directly correspondent to the increase in their mission work. I believe that God makes an EMC grow so that it can do his work. There is an attraction to the excitement of God's call.

It is for the good and faithful servants of the Lord becoming the EMC that I am journaling my testimony. I have witnessed Jesus as our living hope, whose body, the church, is being called upon, now more than ever, to be the salvation of a world in need. In this book I intend to share the excitement of their stories of transformation from the old to the new.

It is my prayer that *The Tale of Two Churches* will be an inspiration to those who are seeking the peace of Christ. It is also my prayer that they may be so moved by the Holy Spirit that they will want to share what they find and become missionaries themselves. Jesus put it this way: "Go home to your friends and tell them how much the Lord has done for you and what mercy he has shown you" (Mark 5:19, NRSV).

I dedicate this book to those of the mission, the EMC that comes to know Christ and makes him known, and then faithfully goes out into the world loving and serving him with all of their hearts.

PART ONE:
The church in Transformation: Becoming EMC

"I can do all things through Christ who strengthens me."
Philippians 4:13, NRSV

CHAPTER ONE:
Today's Church, OCC and EMC

A few years ago at a Bible study I was leading, one of the students asked the group, "Why is the church so divided?" We had just read how Jesus said that he and the Father are one (John 10:30 RSV). The question was a good one. If Jesus asked us to be one, just as He and the Father are one, why do we not follow his instructions?

I liked the way the discussion followed. We agreed that the unity of the church comes in our unity in Christ and that our unity with God the Father comes through Jesus, but at first we failed to come to a conclusion on how we are to be unified with each other when we honestly have differences and disagreements.

Our final thought was that our differences do not mean that we are not united. One person noted that Jesus never said we had to agree, he said we have to love each other. That, we agreed, is much more difficult.

The church has always had its different camps. The divisions sometimes have kept the church from doing its work here on earth, but in other times the divisions have led to greater understanding and, by the power of the Holy Spirit, a renewed faith.

The tale of two churches goes back two thousand years, maybe even further. When Jesus walked the paths of the Holy Land there were two main lines of Jewish teaching, the Law and the Prophets. Jesus came in answer to one and to fulfill the other. The union of the two was completed in the Resurrection and was set into motion as a new relationship with God at Pentecost.

1

The early church quickly divided into two groups, Greeks and Jews. St. Paul came along to unite these two. Later the church divided into east and west, Greek and Latin. That division still remains, although the division has softened into mostly cultural identity rather than theological differences.

Over the centuries there have been endless divisions that have separated Christians from one another. In 1517, Martin Luther published *The Ninety-Five Theses,* not to divide the church, but rather to reform it. With all of his good intentions, the western church was divided into Protestant and Catholic. That division still remains, but it too has softened. Most of Luther's ninety-five points have been generally accepted by Protestants and Catholics alike.

Luther would be so pleased that Roman Catholics today can receive communion in both the Host and the Cup. They sing hymns in worship, as well. Mostly, he would be pleased that the practice of trying to buy your way into heaven through indulgences has faded away. Luther's understanding of salvation by faith alone has become a universal teaching. The Roman Catholic Church has even forgiven Luther and some have praised him for his reforms.

Other divisions have come and gone. My own Anglican tradition had its high and low church liturgical styles. These traditions have led to new denominations such as the Presbyterians, Puritans, and Methodists. Again, these differences have softened. Most mainline churches have become very much alike. The average Presbyterian these days would feel comfortable in any of the other churches and most likely would not know the difference except for a few favorite hymns and some traditional prayers. Today people easily move between one denomination and another. Church leaders are very much aware that today there is very little "denominational brand loyalty," especially among young people.

Today there are differences in churches that I would not call divisions, but rather the diversity of the universal church.

Traditional and contemporary worship, even conservative and liberal theology, are not necessarily divisions in the church but rather are expressions of the faith. It is only when these things become the central focus of a congregation or group of churches that Christian orthodoxy (true belief) is breached and division happens. This is when mission is usually lost.

A friend of mine says that it is when we worship our worship style, or when we worship our political correctness then we are separated from the Body of Christ. I think she is correct. Our biggest problems in the church today happen when we begin to worship an idol, whatever it may be.

There are wonderful liberal-thinking congregations, usually in big cities, that are reaching out to the marginalized. These churches often are a voice for social justice in their communities. They have led the way for human rights and they are in mission to those who suffer in today's urban jungles. They take Christ out into the world so that he will be known to those who would other wise not find him. These are the EMC.

Likewise, there are also wonderful conservative congregations often found in suburban areas which are keeping the faith among those struggling with the complexities of our changing society. They have stood up for family values at a time when families are failing. They are bringing faith values back to people who have lost their way in the secular world. They also make Christ known to many who would not otherwise know his love and grace. These too are the EMC.

I wish that liberals and conservatives would take the time to see the value of the other's role in the greater church. Both are desperately needed.

Finding Common Ground

In May 2009, President Barack Obama addressed the graduates at Notre Dame University in South Bend, Indiana. As he made his remarks he was facing protesters who disagreed with his pro-choice stance on abortions. In a May 18, 2009 *Washington Post* report he was quoted, "As citizens of a vibrant and varied democracy, how do we engage in vigorous debate? How does each of us remain firm in our principles, and fight for what we consider right, without demonizing those with just as strongly held convictions on the other side?" The president posed a great question.

Liberals and conservatives listen to him. We do not need to agree to be in love and charity with each other. Obama went on to say, "Let us find the common ground." In his remarks he suggested, "Let us work together to reduce the number of women seeking abortions."

A Roman Catholic neighbor of mine commented on the president's address. She said, "I like his way of looking at abortion." She added, "I don't agree with him because I am pro-life. That is my religious conviction, but I think what the president is saying is that we should get women to *choose life* not abortion." She looked at me and asked, "Does that make me pro-choice?"

I didn't answer her, but I was thinking to myself that it made her neither. Rather, she is pro-understanding. I think the church could use some pro-understanding these days. We need to find common ground, especially when we have major disagreements. The search for common ground should be a mission of the EMC.

Other EMC Examples

Dealing with another issue of our times, there are exciting congregations, sometimes called *mega churches,* telling the good news of Jesus Christ to a new generation. These are the EMC. Thousands, if not millions, of unchurched people these days are seeking to find meaning in their lives. More than half of those under age thirty do not attend church, yet their generation is searching for something resembling faith. The mission church is answering the call.

Finally, there are growing community churches, such as the one I had the honor of leading, where retired persons are learning how to be disciples alongside young children. These are the missions where everyday people are learning about doing meaningful ministry. These are places where the ministry of the laity is being raised up. Neighbor helping neighbor, friend to friend—the church is learning to do ministry in a very practical way. These also are the EMC.

These community congregations are the churches in the front lines of the battles facing people in the economic downturn of 2008-2009. As the economic downturn has meant the loss of jobs and the loss of homes, the mission church has responded with practical ministries, helping people cope and helping them find practical solutions to their problems. One Lutheran parish in Ohio is helping some people find employment by teaching them new marketable skills at the same time they are teaching about the power of prayer in dealing with problems.

All of these mission-minded congregations are what it means to be the EMC.

The Two Churches of Our Times

The two churches of our times, old chapel churches and emerging missionary churches, view the world very differently. The chapel is the church that looks inward and the mission is the church that looks outward.

The OCC

The OOC is the church of most of the past sixteen hundred years. From the time of Constantine in the fourth century, it has kept the faith and it has been a place of God's love and grace. It has been a chapel, a holy sanctuary where people have come to pray, and, I must point out, it has been true to the faith. The problem is that by its very nature it is unable to meet the demands of the post-modern and post-Christian era, in which just being a place of God's love is not enough to bring new people to the faith. Our times demand more than the chapel can give.

Archbishop William Temple, in the 1940s, told his people in England that the church is the one organization that exists for those who are not yet members. The OCC congregation seldom reaches beyond it own members. I think Temple would understand why this style of church is dying. His words were timely. Since World War II the church of our parents is not necessarily the one we attend.

We quit going to the local OCC, not because it stood for anything we didn't believe or that it wasn't filled with nice people. We stopped going because we became mobile. We went out into the world and we discovered the chapel wasn't relative in the world we live in. It has failed to attract others to Christ. And, for many of us, we married someone from a different style of chapel. The OCC we knew wouldn't do for either of us.

Marks of the OCC:

1. Congregations look inward and are centered on their own existence.
2. They fondly remember the past, ignore the present, and fear the future.
3. They feel helpless and hopeless.
4. They are declining in ministries, members, and attendance.

The EMC

The EMC, on the other hand, is thriving. It thrives because it reaches out to all people, it ministers to those in need, it cares about bringing the faith to a world in chaos, it is energized by its diversity, and it understands that the great commandment to love and the great commission to bring the faith to all nations are the callings of the mission. The EMC upholds the orthodox

Christian faith and the eternal truth of God's word. What is orthodox and true is that the church must be in mission to lead others to Christ.

The EMC is the church growing to meet the complexities of the post-modern world. It is fully engaged in the mission of the church. The central task of the EMC is to lead others to Christ, help them grow in the Lord, and then to send them out to lead others in the same way. It is being led by the Holy Spirit, emerging to its full potential for our challenging times.

A Mission For Our Times

We now live in a world that cannot be considered Christian even in places where Christianity is still the major religion. We have become a global society where we live next door to someone who is probably from another geographic area and most likely has a different religious belief. The old Polish neighborhood where my wife grew up, and the German neighborhood I knew, no longer exists. In today's world it is the EMC that can bring order to the chaos of a society that has turned to secularism when the chapel failed.

The 2008 study by the Pew Forum on Religion and Public Life offered an interesting conclusion to their 36,000-person survey. They noted that most people (about ninety percent) believe in God and that most people observe a moral code based on basic religious principles, but more than half have no loyalty to a particular denomination. Most have a variety of religious beliefs not grounded in a particular tradition.

A 2009 AOL News poll with more than 90,000 responding shows that seventy-two percent of the people in the United States call themselves Christians, yet only one in four of them regularly attend a church.

It is interesting to note that denominational loyalty has continued to decline for several decades. Back in the '80s and '90s, author and professor Wade Clark Roof studied the religious traditions of the generations since World War II. He found a rapid change in the way people viewed their traditions. Denominational loyalty in the '80s was already on the decline, but in the years since Roof's study disloyalty is becoming the norm.

When I read the words of the Prophet Isaiah, I can't help but feel that he was writing about our times as well as his own when he noted how his generation abandoned their faith, lost their temple, and were exiled to Babylon. His words have eternal truth. But the good news is that the prophet saw hope for the people of Israel; after all, they were God's chosen people. In time God led them back into his good grace. The same hope is ours. If we are faithful and follow, God will lead us back to where he wants us to be.

Today, religious formation is often based on secular values shaped around people's own ethical beliefs. For most, the hope of their future is a personal thing and the salvation of their soul is something they do not understand at all. Like the people of Isaiah's time, many today are wandering in exile from a temple they never knew.

It is for these people that the EMC is so important. One can not be in communion with God and neighbor by one's self. The community of faith is not about being a place where one comes to pray alone. It is about coming to know Christ in a communion of faith and then becoming one of his followers (a disciple) who enters into a union with other believers to be the Body of Christ, doing God's work here on earth. This is the mission of the EMC.

Marks of the EMC:

1. Congregations look outward for opportunities to serve in the name of Christ.
2. They join together to seek ways to ways to lead others to Christ. They share God's love in formation, worship, prayer, ministry, and evangelism.

3. They look to the future with optimism.
4. They are increasing the ministries they offer. Membership and attendance are growing.

The Mission Church in Books

A long list of wonderful books has been written about the mission church. Pastor Rick Warren of the Saddleback Community Church in Orange County, California, wrote the definitive book on the subject, *The Purpose Driven Church* (Zondervan, 1995). In it he cites: fellowship, discipleship, worship, ministry, and evangelism as the keys to the mission church's purpose. He calls for people to be transformed. He offers what he calls the five circles of commitment from people who come into the church. They are: 1. reaching out to the *community* of the unchurched; 2. bringing them into *membership*; 3. forming them into a *congregation* of regular members; 4. getting them to be *committed*; 5. and empowering what he calls the *core members*. The subtitle of his book is, "Growth Without Compromising Your Message and Mission." He holds up the basics of the Christian faith in calling for mission.

Warren has contributed to the transformation of the church from chapel to mission. His more recent best seller, *The Purpose Driven Life* (Zondervan, 2002), deals with personal transformation. Both books have changed lives.

I will not try to redo what Warren and others have done so well. Rather I will reflect from personal experience on what the mission of the EMC means to the person in the pew and the disciple out in the mission field. As congregations have been transformed from chapel to mission I have witnessed the transformation of people. People's lives have been renewed and they have entered into the Peace of Christ through the power of the Holy Spirit simply because their congregations have become empowered to be missionaries.

A Woman Made New

This is the story of a person in the pew who was made new through the love of Christ shown at an EMC. For her privacy we will just call her Rose.

One Sunday I was filling in at a parish while the priest in charge was on vacation. Usually at times like these a visiting priest only gets to visit casually with the people. This could have been one of those times except for a woman I cannot forget.

Rose was not a regular at this particular church, but I didn't know that. She came up to me after the service and asked if she could have a word in private. This happens often to clergy; people have the opportunity to see you on Sunday and they want to talk. After shaking hands with a long line of people, I suggested to Rose that we share some coffee. We took our cups and sat at a table in the parish hall a few feet away from the rest of the people. She couldn't wait to tell me her troubles.

Rose was homeless and desperate for help. What she seemed to need most was a bath; one couldn't miss that. Then she seemed to be hungry. I got her a sandwich. After talking for a few minutes I could tell that someone was going to have to get Rose to a shelter or someplace where she could get the assistance she needed. The church needed to take care of her personal needs before we could deal with her soul.

The woman in charge of the altar guild asked me if there was anything I needed. I told her I was fine, but this woman, Rose, needed some assistance. She looked at her and saw what I meant. I could tell she was not comfortable with the situation, but I could also tell she cared. She called to another woman who came over; she was ready to help. The second lady was in charge of the parish outreach ministry. She knew the people over at the local homeless shelter. Within a few minutes we had someone to pick up Rose and take her to a place where she could be helped.

I returned to the church the next Sunday to fill in again and the outreach lady came running over to me to let me know what had happened to the homeless woman. It seems that Rose was not just another homeless person. She was the daughter of a prominent local family. She had been in an abusive situation with her boyfriend and she had nowhere to go. She was on drugs and she was afraid to go home to her parents.

Some weeks later I learned that the chaplain at the shelter was also the pastor of another local church. The chaplain and the outreach lady teamed up to work with Rose. They got her into a drug rehab program and a safe environment. They got her to reconcile with her family and they got her to church. It was at church that she made the most progress. The chaplain felt that it was appropriate that Rose return to the church that sent her, so the outreach lady became her new chaplain. Rose became friends with her new lay pastor and others at her new church home.

When I returned the next summer to again fill in for the same priest, I was reintroduced to Rose. I didn't recognize her. She was nicely dressed, clean, and I could tell she was very intelligent. Her smile brightened her face. She was glowing with something new. As we talked I could tell that the Holy Spirit had lifted this person up from the pit and delivered her to the world as a new person. Rose was transformed, and the EMC led the way.

This is the EMC at its best. It is the church reaching out in love to live out the great commandment to love our neighbors. It is the church caring enough to lead someone to the peace of Christ.

I will never forget Rose and I'm sure she will never forget the place where she found God's loving kindness.

Chapter One Essentials:

1. The chapel (OCC) looks inward and the mission (EMC) looks out into the world.
2. The world we live in has changed so much that the OCC is no longer able to do its ministry effectively.
3. The Holy Spirit is leading the church to its mission through congregations that are emerging as missionaries.
4. People are being touched by God and transformed as new people through the EMC.

Chapter One Question:

What ministries in your congregation are OCC, and what are EMC? How far has your congregation come toward being an EMC?

"He did it with all his heart, and prospered."
2 Chronicles 31:21, NRSV

CHAPTER TWO:
The Power of the EMC

While traveling to Uganda via England in the summer of 2000, my wife Janet and I had the good fortune to visit some very interesting churches. In addition to visiting Canterbury Cathedral and other historic places in England, we attended Sunday worship at St. John the Baptist Church in the Kensington section of London.

The sign in front of the church was something I could not resist. It read, "High Mass 11 A.M." We showed up at about five minutes to eleven and we were the only people in the church. I wondered if the time had been changed for the summer. At eleven, a few others entered the church. The bells rang and a few more entered. The clergy and altar party processed to their places. Counting everyone there were twelve people. I looked over at Janet and asked, "What is going on here?"

The service was fine and the sermon was fair, but I came away depressed at seeing only twelve people in a five hundred-seat church.

A week later we were in Kisoro, Uganda, to take part in the Jubilee Celebration of the Diocese of Muhabura at St. Andrew's Cathedral in that remote part of east Africa. This is a town which is fifty miles past the end of a paved road.

I was privileged to take part in the Sunday worship. A procession of more than one hundred fifty clergy and lay leaders marched from the diocesan offices down a dusty packed-cinder road to the cathedral. At the door of the twelve hundred-seat church a crowd waited for a liturgy which included the blessing of the church building by the Archbishop of Uganda. Then the procession marched to an outdoor area where more than five thousand people were waiting. The main part of the worship had to be held outside because of the crowd.

I was struck by the contrast. This time both Janet and I commented that there was energy in Kisoro that was missing in London.

One week we visited a church in London that stated in its bulletin that it was dedicated to the "Preservation of Holy Worship" and the next week we visited one that quoted St. Paul, proclaiming, "Jesus is our living hope." I do not mean to say that St. John the Baptist is typical of the Church of England. There are many great mission-minded congregations there. And I do not mean to say that the beauty of holiness is not important. The real issue for me is the reason for the existence of that church in London. St. John's was a chapel, there to preserve the past, and the mission for the cathedral in Kisoro is to proclaim the good news of Jesus Christ.

My experience at these two churches, of course, offers examples at the far ends of the spectrum of congregational life. To be sure, St. Andrew's Cathedral does not hold a Jubilee Celebration every Sunday. However, more than a thousand people regularly call St. Andrew's their church home.

My various studies in congregational development have taught me that this experience is somewhat of a parable illustrating the differences in the two types of churches and in the changing nature of the church today.

The OCC is clinging to the past, or it is at least slumbering happily in an ever-shrinking comfort zone. The chapel is seeing its people leave in a constant line out the door. The chapel's numbers are declining and its future is bleak. The empty OCC, such as St. John's in London, is the sad result.

The EMC is energized and growing. As a group, the mission churches are struggling with the changes in today's world, but they are finding hope in the power of the Resurrection. The mission church is not a totally new church; it is the apostolic church that is renewed and now emerging by the power of the Holy Spirit. St. Andrew's Cathedral in Uganda is a fine example of the EMC.

Learning from the Developing World

Because change is always difficult, the pioneering EMC is far from a comfort zone, yet there is joy. These latter day apostles are finding ways to reach past their own boundaries into a world desperately seeking spiritual connections. In east Africa, in the United States, and in places in between, there is a renewal of the faith being brought to people in need by a church in mission.

What were once remote missionary outposts in the Christian world are now returning the mission to those who once gave it. The missionary heritage of people in the developing world is now being called upon to share the mission with the very nations who sent them the faith. African and Asian missionaries are found in North America and in Europe these days. Their valuable understanding of mission is desperately needed by the OCC trying to find its way to mission.

The universal church today finds itself in a non-Christian world. Much like the church prior to Emperor Constantine, today's church finds itself in a missionary field where most of the people are marginal Christians or are not Christian at all.

People these days do not just come to a church because it is there. Most people today have very little knowledge about what goes on inside the walls of a church building, or if they do, they might have serious doubts about the value of what is going on inside. If all the church is doing within its walls is self-serving, the doubts may be well founded.

In a world where people hardly know the Christian story it is the EMC that is called to tell that story. Our times demand more than a chapel church can give. The church today must not only tell the Christian story, but it must live it out. It must make that story what I call a *credo in action*. Our call is to take what we believe, *our creed*, and put it into motion. This requires a major shift in the way the church thinks and acts out its ministry.

The church of today, particularly the decision-making authority of mainline denominations, is being called to transform its congregations to mission. Retired Episcopal Bishop Claude Payne of Texas, in his book, *Reclaiming the Great Commission*, written with Hamilton Beazley (Jossey-Bass, 2000), has called this work the development of missionary outposts. He calls for the transformation of congregations and people to experience spiritual growth and what he calls "miraculous expectations." Payne proclaims that if you are in mission you can expect miracles.

Sadly, most mainline denominations have failed to understand the EMC. The Episcopal Church, my own denomination, has failed time and time again. Most Episcopal congregations are the OCC in decline. Today, half of Episcopal congregations have less than seventy attending on Sunday.

My tradition of the church has been acting as if it was in mission, but it is returning to the chapel at every chance. There was the Decade of Evangelism (the '90s) when the Episcopal Church said it was seeking new members, but it lost members. Then there was the effort to double the size of the church by the year 2020. According to 2007 Episcopal Church research, it is now losing more than 750 members a week. The mission goal has faded away.

What is wrong? The problem is not only the issues of the day, but rather the lack of mission that has resulted from a preoccupied denomination. The preoccupation with a single issue, human sexuality, has taken away most interest in the mission church and has pushed the Episcopal Church into a downward cycle. Good and faithful Episcopalians on all sides of this issue have forgotten the church's mission. This is the basic reason why so many have left this once great expression of the Christian faith. Other denominations have faced similar situations.

At this point, if I did not address the issue of homosexuality, I would be ignoring the elephant in the living room. This single issue has divided all of the Christian faith. Every major expression of Christianity is dealing with the understanding of homosexuality. Feelings are at a fever pitch. My denomination stands at ground zero of this battle.

As I see it, there are two issues here, the issue of civil rights and the issue of faith. As a minister of the church I must conform to the laws of the state and the canons of the church, but what is the emperor's is the emperor's, and what is God's is God's. I personally feel that the civil rights of gay and lesbian people call out for civil justice. On the other hand, the faith community must look at the issue from a far different perspective.

For me, the call to minister to gay and lesbian people is truly what Jesus would do. He always reached out to the marginalized. Our baptismal vows tell us to uphold the dignity of every human being. There is the clear pastoral reason for the church, particularly the EMC, to minister to this community.

For many, however, the authority of Scripture speaks clearly. The church must uphold what is right and what is wrong, based on the foundation of Scriptural authority. To those holding this view, homosexuality is a sin. Struggling with this is also a calling of the mission church.

The debate is far from over. For me, prayer and study are the answer. I agree that we must minister to all people; yes, that is what Jesus would do. Yet on the other hand, I cannot, as a priest and minister of the gospel, bless the union of a same-sex couple. I must be a pastor to them, but I cannot bless them as I would bless a man and woman in Holy Matrimony. The change of state laws will only make this issue more difficult.

The biblical authority for my opinion is not just found in the books of Moses or in the teachings of St. Paul, which speak about homosexuality. Of course these are not to be taken lightly. For me, however, the struggle is about understanding God's life giving creation. I look to the words of Jesus (Matt. 19:5) when he quoted the creation story in Genesis (Gen. 2:24), saying that marriage is between a man and a woman: "They become one flesh." I am not proof texting here—that is using an out-of-context passage from Scripture to prove a point—but rather I am using the basic truth from creation which Jesus taught.

Faithfully, I continue to study.

The sacraments, rites, and rituals of the church are not mine to change. The universal church led by the Holy Spirit must be the decision-maker. Holy Scripture must be our foundation. Only God knows if I am right or wrong. It is my prayer that the collective mind of the church, led by the Holy Spirit, will someday give us God's answer. I think most Christians struggle with this issue in the same way. In the meantime, I cannot change what is not mine to change.

If I were a gay person, I'm sure I would think differently. It is only through prayer and study that we as a universal church will be able to come to grips with this situation that divides us so deeply. This issue, more than any other is keeping my denomination and most of the Christian church from its mission.

It is my personal prayer that the Episcopal Church, which I love deeply, will find itself and return to its mission. All of the EMC must find itself in prayer on this. Then I pray that the Episcopal Church and its Anglican brothers and sisters will lead the way in this issue in a faithful manner, being true to the authority of Scripture with faithful pastoral care for one another. Then we can become the church God wants it to be—a church in mission.

OCC to EMC

With some notable exceptions, most mainline Protestant denominations are turning over the struggle to become mission-minded to their parish congregations. Some judicatories (diocese, presbyteries, conferences, districts, and synods) are offering training to their congregations on becoming the EMC. Bishop

Dabney Smith of my diocese in Florida has been a good example of how a regional leader can assist congregations to be the EMC. My bishop and his staff have introduced several good training courses and programs, including Fresh Start, Total Ministries and the Start Up, Start Over. These are programs for leaders, both lay and ordained. These and other programs used in other areas are designed to move congregations into mission.

Sadly, this is an exception in my tradition. My diocese is one of a very few deeply committed to being the EMC. Most are leaving the task up to their individual congregations. I think this is passing the buck. Leadership for most of the OCC is lacking. Meanwhile, chapel congregations are failing, one after another.

In the context of our changing world, congregations today must, mostly on their own, move past the ancient chapel model where everyone was assumed to be Christian and where people simply came to church. The new post-Christian world requires the new model of church.

An Example of the EMC

The church in east Africa is a fine example of the EMC, as evidenced by my experience at St. Andrew's Cathedral. That mission-minded cathedral is dedicated to outreach and evangelism. This model of faith which I witnessed in Uganda is growing because it is ministering to its people.

When I first traveled to Kisoro, Uganda, in 1998 the people there had just started to get electrical power. Telephones were rare and television was only viewed in Kampala, the capital, three hundred miles away. When I visited two years later, electrical power was reaching many more people in Kisoro and cellular telephones were everywhere. Today television dish receivers are found in many places and CNN and the BBC are widely viewed.

In a matter of one decade the people of this remote place were brought into the new century with instant communication.

Their lives will never be the same. It is hard to say what will happen because of this change, but things will change for sure. After suffering under harsh dictators in primitive conditions, these people are now witnesses to the election of a black man as President of the United States of America, a man whose father came from neighboring Kenya. They have become part of the global community. There is a new confidence among the people of Uganda. Their hearts are filled with hope for the future.

The need for their faith has never been greater. With technology being introduced to people who need to learn to use it, with the changes in communications that sometimes offer temptations not known in the past, and with the problem of the orphans left alone due to the AIDS epidemic, the foundation of faith is essential to the stability of the Ugandan society.

Faith has carried the people of Uganda through incredible struggles in the past, and it will again. "God's amazing grace," as one Ugandan told me, "has carried us thus far and it will carry us home." In spite of all of their challenges, these faithful people know God loves them.

The people of east Africa are not baby Christians. The Christian faith was brought to the continent in the late 1800s by English missionary societies that established a church. James Hannington, a missionary priest of the Church of England, became the first bishop of Eastern Africa in 1884. The Anglican Church of Uganda has always been a mission church. It was born EMC, and it has remained.

Today it is the largest denomination in the country (with more than eight million members) and today its leaders are all native born. Hospitals, schools, and colleges all are ministries of the Anglican Church of Uganda. It has more members than all of the Anglicans in North and South America combined. Uganda is the most Christian nation on earth. More than ninety percent of its people are Christian, mostly Anglican and Roman Catholic.

The issue of homosexuality has estranged the Church of Uganda from the American Episcopal Church. The issue is particularly deep-rooted there. The history of the conversion of the Ugandan people to Christianity began with the example of martyrs in 1885. Legend has it that a group of thirty-three Christian men refused to submit to Ugandan King Mwanga's soldiers because of their faith. They were asked to renounce their faith. They would not. It is said that they went to their deaths keeping their faith and singing hymns. Word of this faithfulness spread among the people, bringing large numbers of converts to Christianity. The Martyrs of Uganda are remembered in a national holiday each June 3.

The American Church doesn't understand this. On the other hand, Ugandans don't understand the Americans either.

It is a shame that one issue divides us because there is so much we can learn from each other. The church in east Africa is a fine example of the EMC. It is relevant to the needs of the people, it is faithful to the work it is called to do, and it considers Jesus its living hope.

The power of this mission church is the example we should study. It is difficult for some of us in the West to understand that people in other places and in other times had to risk their lives to be Christian. The early church suffered under harsh Roman law. Being a Christian was not good for your health. Likewise, in Uganda being Christian has not always safe. Under the harsh military rule of Idi Amin, thousands of latter-day Ugandan martyrs have lost their lives for being Christian. In spite of it all, their faith has only grown stronger.

As I stood among the people of Kisoro on one of my visits, I was reminded that many people there knew others who lost their lives for their faith. It is humbling for an American who sometimes takes his faith for granted to be among people who have risked their lives to be Christians.

This is the power of the EMC. The Holy Spirit delivers it, when all else fails. All of us must learn from this church in mission.

A Model for Mission and Ministry

My dear friend Bishop Ernest Shalita, the retired bishop of the Diocese of Muhabura in Uganda, has taught me a great deal about the power that is unleashed through the Holy Spirit in the EMC. His ministry is an example of mission and one we should study.

Ernest Shalita was born in Kisoro to a good and faithful Christian family. He studied hard at their urging. He learned English so he could further his studies. The local church leaders and his family motivated him to go to college and seminary in Uganda and later in England and the United States. The mission church had led him to enter the ministry.

He returned to his country to serve as a priest. His leadership took him to serve his national church as treasurer and as Dean of the National Cathedral in Kampala. It was at the cathedral, in 1977, where he nearly became a martyr himself.

One day while he was inside the cathedral church building, Archbishop Janani Luwum was out in the courtyard. Shots were fired and the leader of the Church of Uganda had become another martyr. Shalita's life was in danger. He managed to find his way to safety, but the memory of that horrible day still lives with him. His deep faith in God, lived out through the power in the EMC, carried him through it all.

Ernest Shalita has lived so that he might do great things. He became bishop in his old hometown where much work was needed. He became chief pastor to eighty thousand people. We met while he was busy in this ministry, making a difference in the lives of people he knew all his life.

"The power of the mission church is the power of the Risen Christ," Bishop Shalita once told me. I was witness to this power. On my first trip to Kisoro I saw the beginning of construction of a village for Batwaw people, the poorest of the poor in east Africa. These people are outcast by most other Africans, yet my friend ministered to them. Tribal and ethnic differences are a serious problem in most of Africa. The bishop has told me more than once, "These people have the potential of every human being." He once wrote, "We must help them. God demands it."

When I made my next trip to Uganda, my wife and I were honored to visit the completed village. The pride these people had in their new homes was only surpassed by the faith they showed. While we visited, they offered prayers for the blessings from God, the good work of the church, and in particular, thanks for their dear bishop.

I also witnessed the building of a residential youth center, a church-sponsored vocational training center, and new health-care facilities. All of this was done in one of the poorest places on earth.

Today Bishop Shalita is retired from diocesan leadership, but his ministry is still in full swing. He has told me that the issues of human sexuality that divide the church are part of his study and prayer life. He is prayerfully seeking answers. Meanwhile, he leads a local program to help AIDS orphans and he travels extensively, raising money through African Team Ministries to support the work of the church in east Africa. The bishop has written twelve books about his work.

Don't ever tell my friend Bishop Ernest Shalita that something cannot be done. He knows where the power is kept. He knows that the Holy Spirit turns on the energy for the church in mission to do its work. Bishop Shalita is the very model of the EMC bishop.

Chapter Two Essentials:

1. The EMC is ordained by Jesus to take the church to all nations and is empowered by the Holy Spirit.
2. The EMC is the church offering the hope of Christ to the world. The OCC is holding on to its past.
3. The EMC must prayerfully deal with divisive issues so that it can refocus on its mission.
4. The emerging church is learning form the missionary experience of the developing world.

Chapter Two Question:

How is your congregation offering the hope of Christ to people beyond your doors?

"God is our refuge and strength, a very present help in trouble." Psalm 46:1, RSV

CHAPTER THREE:
The Holy Decline of the OCC

On Sunday, May 17, 2009, the final worship services were held at the 109-year-old First Christian Church in the historic Hyde Park neighborhood of Tampa, Florida. The beautiful gothic church, which had once been home to more than two thousand worshipers, was about to be sold to another congregation. The aging congregation of First Christian had dwindled to a few hundred people who could no longer financially support the 36,000-square-foot facility in central Tampa. The ministry of another OCC had ended.

I talked to a man I'll call Earl, who had been a member of the congregation for all of his eighty-plus years. "I can't understand what happened to my beloved church," he declared. Like many others he was baptized there and married there. Earl told me that some in that congregation had sent their spouses to their final resting place from the same church were they grew up.

Earl, like thousands, if not millions of other people, wrestles with the same thought. What has happened to my church? Historic OCC congregations like First Christian, and like the one Janet and I visited in London, are part of the great line of chapel churches that for centuries have been a place of comfort to people like Earl. *The New York Times* reported on May 17, 2009 that Our Lady Queen of Angels Church in East Harlem closed two years ago, and yet, still to this day, dozens of people gather on the sidewalk in front of the empty church for Sunday worship. The comfort of these chapels is deeply missed.

To tell Earl that the world has changed and that there is no place for his beloved chapel would be cruel. Particularly among the elderly who grew up in the OCC, the loss is grievous. I have witnessed what this loss has meant to many people. One of my own parishioners once asked me, "Will my church be there when it is time for my funeral?" His doubt is real.

For Earl and his many brothers and sisters in the OCC, the mission church has a moral obligation to reach out in love and compassion. These faithful Christians need Christian love now more than ever. It is the responsibility of the EMC to minister to every person in need, and these people are in need. I will keep Earl in my prayers.

In the greater picture of things, the First Christian building was going to continue as a Christian church. It will become Holy Trinity Presbyterian, a growing mission-minded congregation. Earl's church facility was not going to be torn down as many old historic churches have been and his congregation was moving to smaller quarters. Hopefully in their new place a renewal will take place. There is hope for Earl and the multitudes like him. Although the journey is sometimes difficult, God leads us to renewal. That is the power of the Risen Christ.

"God Makes Things Right"

The Christian Church has fallen from its mission many times in its history. It has fallen short of its mission and it has sinned against God. But in the end, God corrects us, we reconcile, and God, in his mercy, makes things right. The church has been renewed and restored again and again. Each time it is made new, it is different. The changes in the church today are a prime example. The church must always be true to the faith, but to live out that faith it also must be made new. By God's grace, the EMC will be new and it will be different.

From the Ashes

Back in 1994, when I first went to work in the office of the bishop in San Diego, I was serving as editor of the diocesan newspaper, *The Church Times*. One day the phone rang and the man on the other end shouted as if I couldn't hear, "St. John's Church is on fire." I asked which St. John's, since the diocese had several churches with that name. The man hung up.

I went to another office where there was a television and turned it on to see if there was any news. There was none. So I turned on my radio. Sure enough, the all-news station had a live report from St. John's Episcopal Church in Chula Vista, California, where the sanctuary was ablaze. I ran to my car and headed to St. John's.

When I arrived the fire was almost out. Fire crews were mopping up. People were standing there stunned. One lady had her face in her hands in total silence. Others were crying. One woman sobbed, "What will we do now that our church is gone?" This was more than the loss of a building; the place where faith, hope, and love were found was gone. One could not help but feel that it was hopeless. The church was burned to the ground. It was a Good Friday moment for sure.

Later that day I interviewed the rector, the Rev. Michael Kaehr. Michael was sad to be sure, but he lifted his voice and proclaimed, "Gods makes things right." That was the headline I used in the newspaper.

Almost three years later, at the dedication of the beautiful new St. John's Church, I leaned over to Michael Kaehr and whispered, "God makes things right." He understood what I meant. Of course, this was the Easter moment.

When all seems lost, when we are at our darkest moments, the power of the Holy Spirit is there for us. From the ashes of St. John's came the beautiful new church facility where several years later Episcopal Presiding Bishop Frank Griswold filmed a video for the Episcopal Church. As I watched the presiding bishop speak to the camera in front of the new baptismal font inside the new St. John's, I had to remember that "God makes things right."

Many people today remind me of those standing before the ashes of St. John's. As many mainline churches appear to be in ashes, some are crying like the lady in Chula Vista: "What will we do now that our church is gone?"

God makes things right. The power of the Risen Christ has renewed Christians for two thousand years. Through century after century of wars and conflict, through good times and bad times, through every struggle known to the human race, God has made things right. The holy catholic church has survived and grown. We can be confident that God will take the OCC and make the EMC from it. From the ashes will come the new.

I must quote from the beautiful words used in prayer at ordinations: "Let the whole world see and know that things which were cast down are being raised up, that things which had grown old are being made new, and that all things are being brought to their perfection by him through whom all things were made, your Son Jesus Christ our Lord" (*Book of Common Prayer*, p. 540).

The OCC may have come to the end of its days, but the holy catholic church is alive and well. The EMC will replace it. The church is not going to be dead; resurrection for the faithful will take place. But resurrection means new and different life. What has grown old is being made new and different. This is the power of the Resurrection happening right before our eyes.

The Rev. Charles N. Fulton III, creator of the Start Up, Start Over program in the Episcopal Church, holds that the power of the Resurrection is the hope of the congregational renewal movement. Fulton challenges congregations to "rediscover the optimistic, mission-minded spirit that marks healthy and thriving congregations." He teaches that all congregations can be made new by the power of the Risen Christ.

Mike Regele in his book, *Death of the Church* (Zondervan, 1995), observed that demise of chapel churches is part of the process of the renewal of the whole church. Regele calls on church leaders to champion mission churches and to do the careful work necessary to bring congregations from the old model to the new.

What he and other congregational development experts have been saying for at least twenty years is that the church is being called to change, but the people are going to have to answer the call. God may make things right, but it will be human hands that will do the heavy lifting.

Changing the church is a cleansing act. Like rebuilding St. John's we are now being called to rebuild the church. When things grow old, as even people do, we must find newness. The wonder of the Resurrection is not only the promise of eternal life, but is also the promise of new life here and now. This is transformation.

A New Season in the Church

While I served on the staff of Bishop Gethin Hughes in San Diego, I learned the meaning of the word *transformation*. My friend Gethin, a deeply mission-minded servant of God, came to me one day and said, "I want to start a program to change the diocesan focus to mission and ministry." Several years earlier he had held a diocesan convention where he handed out M&M candies to remind people of mission and ministry. I have seen that done several times since. He had asked the diocese on several occasions to move into mission, but many did not respond. Change is always difficult.

The bishop was now asking his staff to take action. He told me that he wanted to start what he called a "season" where people would be transformed from where they were to the mission they were called to do. The program became called "The Season of Transformation." I had the honor of serving in a leadership role in this program.

The important part of this effort was our call for small congregations to reach their potential. It was also a call for larger congregations to expand their ministries and do new things. Most of the diocesan churches responded and there was an excitement among the people. I saw congregations of forty people become four hundred. I witnessed major congregations enter into bold building programs after which several new churches were built. There was a power turned on and good things began to happen. Bishop Hughes was right, transformed people can make a difference.

It has been my observation that even though people are resistant to change, when they see the power of the EMC there is a natural desire to be part of what is new and exciting. People in the comfort of a chapel can easily be motivated to the excitement of the mission, if they are only given the chance.

A pastor in a church in Michigan told me that when his congregation began reaching out in mission, people began to volunteer to do things. "Some of these people never did anything before, but now there is excitement," he said.

The OCC is in the final days of its life cycle. It is a holy decline, because God has the need for a new mission. The EMC must become the new way we exercise our faith. The congregations where we have dwelled must be transformed from one to the other, made new and different to answer God's call.

Chapter Three Essentials:

1. As the OCC declines, God is making the church new.
2. God always makes things right.
3. The power of the Resurrection brings new life.
4. The new emerging church, through the power of the Holy Spirit, is transforming people's lives.

Chapter Three Questions:

What is your congregation doing to be transformed into something new? How does your congregation act on our Christian belief that the Resurrection defeats death?

PART TWO:
The Mission is in Our hands

"If you know these things, you are blessed if you do them."
John 13:17, RSV

CHAPTER FOUR:
EMC, Education of the Faithful: Christian Formation

For several months I spent a few afternoons a week visiting an elderly parishioner in hospice. Her name was Marion Burk, and in her interesting way she was one of my heroes. At age eighty-seven, she still wanted to learn.

One day she asked me to read to her a Gospel lesson we had discussed once in a class. It was the story of the woman at the well from John (John 4:7). Marion had taken my short course on the Fourth Gospel and she had a particular interest in this lesson. What impressed me about our conversation was that a woman who only had a few weeks left in her earthly journey still wanted to study and learn.

"What did Jesus mean by living water?" Marion asked. We got into a discussion about baptism and about her life in Christ. She taught me a thing or two. First, Marion was a great example of a disciple. She understood that, like the woman at the well, Jesus knew her. Her life as a Christian was a communion between her and our Lord and a similar union with all those she knew. She had loved and served the Lord all of her life, but second, and just as important, Marion always had a question. She wanted to learn and grow even in her final days. For that, she was my hero.

After she died, the people of St. Martin's dedicated the new brick walkway to the front of the church in her memory. It is now known as the Marion Burk Inspirational Walk. She was an inspiration. I hope that her legacy for all of us is a desire to learn.

Our Christian formation is a lifelong journey. The EMC depends on this kind of learning for its energy. Teaching is an essential part of Jesus' great commission. He said, "...*teaching* them all that I have commanded you." Part of the mission of the church is to prepare the saints for ministry. Learning at every age is essential.

For many, unlike Marion Burk, the learning journey ends at the last day of Sunday school, or at our Confirmation. A bishop I know once told those he was confirming that "Confirmation is not graduation." Indeed, learning is a lifelong process, yet the OCC is often guilty of ending the process at about age fourteen.

Fortunately for people like Marion there are opportunities to learn even at the hospice house where she spent her final days. It is the responsibility of the church to help people grow in every phase of their life. The EMC has learned to continue the learning process at every stage. From teenage coming-of-age programs and young adult ministries, to adult classes and renewal ministries, the EMC is actively seeking ways to help people grow in their faith.

We are all works in progress and God isn't finished with any of us yet. Every person, at any age can still learn something and grow. That is one of the wonders of life. There is always something to learn that will make us more complete as human beings. For this reason the EMC has put great emphasis on what is now being called "Christian formation."

Over the past several years I have witnessed several styles of teaching that have helped me and my flock. We have learned to be good students of our faith. First and foremost, all learning should be interesting, if not downright fun.

The OCC method was to drill things into our heads with repetition. As a student in this system, I did commit several passages of Scripture to memory, but I failed to learn much about what they meant. In some instances the old chapel even allowed child abuse in the name of learning. Nuns and their rulers, I'm afraid, were part of the OCC.

It has been my experience that learning includes understanding, so just committing things to memory is not real learning. On the other hand, just playing games about learning is not learning either. There is still a discipline required in gaining knowledge.

The EMC is constantly experimenting with ways to teach, as it should. With a new generation today that has grown up with computers, a whole new style of instruction is being introduced. Just as visuals were important to their parents who grew up with television, computers and their capacity to inform are a new source of information dissemination. But, no matter what the medium, a focus on understanding and experience in an orderly fashion is the basic method necessary in the mission church. Students must experience the lesson in real ways that they can understand.

An Experience Not to Be Forgotten

St. Martin's was planning a Vacation Bible School (VBS) one summer and the typical games and storytelling were being tossed around. The year before only a handful of children registered, so I thought something new would be appropriate.

Sometimes God gives us epiphanies just when we need them. I was at a meeting of my Rotary Club when the guest speaker was from the local animal rescue center. I was fascinated how the woman explained the method for rehabilitating birds and other animals so that they could be returned to the wild. She said, "God gave us dominion over the animals, which means we have a responsibility to take care of them."

A light bulb when off in my head. The children would love this. So I hurried back to the church and called the two people helping to plan our VBS. They agreed that a trip to the animal rescue center would be a wonderful experience, so we got to work. We talked to some of the children to see what they thought. They were interested. Then we brainstormed as to what we would be teaching in our program. The answer was given to us by the lady from the center: "God gave us dominion over the animals" (Gen 1:28, RSV).

Our VBS would be about the creation story and about how human beings have a responsibility to care for all of God's creations. We found films from the Nature Channel and from Disney about the animals we would be seeing at the shelter. We found Web sites on human responsibility for animals. Then we read from Genesis and studied the days of creation as the eras of the development of nature. We discussed the responsibility of taking care of all of God's creations.

At the rescue center we were able to hold some of the animals. One of the dads got to hold a bird that would later that day be released into the wild. It was a good thing that his daughter didn't hold that particular animal. Dad had to wash his hands while learning about nature. The youngsters did get to hold some baby raccoons. No messes there.

The experience was wonderful. We had a good group of energetic young people who wanted to take part. They wanted to learn and they came away with an experience that I know they will not forget. We used written material, visuals, the Internet, and actual hands-on experience to teach and learn. Learning was interesting and it was fun, but most important it taught a whole variety of lessons. Every one of us, adults and children alike, grew from our experience.

This is EMC Christian formation at its best. This is the creative, multimedia style of teaching that the mission church of today is being called to do. At every level, when learning is interesting, it helps people grow in their faith.

Biblical Literacy

Early in my ministry I learned that many people lack even a basic knowledge of the Bible. I have found that this biblical ignorance is not just found among un-churched people, but among those who attend church regularly in most denominations. I have often wondered to myself, do they listen to sermons? I think they do, if they are interesting, but sometimes they don't know what we're talking about. I have learned to be careful not to assume that people know the lesson from which I am preaching.

Most people in the pews know that Moses was a leader of God's chosen people and they know, but often do not understand, why Jesus was born to the Virgin Mary. Beyond this they only know a few stories like Noah's Ark, the Christ Child and the wise men, and Jesus walking on water. They might remember last week's sermon … maybe. For many, biblical stories just seem confusing. Too often, people try to learn biblical lessons using literal understanding. This causes their confusion. They should look deeper into the words and study them to find the eternal truth of God's inspired words.

In the past hundred years biblical scholarship has come a long way. Studies into the context and history of biblical passages have led to new and deeper understandings of God's word. The study of the Scriptures with a literary understanding has given the world a more poetic look at eternal truth. For me the Psalms have come alive when I read them as the songs they were meant to be.

But for all this good work, the average person has become less informed about the Scriptures. I think that the scholars should have taken more time to smell the roses. They should have spent more time using their research to find a deeper understanding of the good news of Jesus Christ. We should always study and seek the truth, but we have to put the truth into action somewhere along the line. Of course, that is the job of the pastoral teacher and preacher.

If the church is to be in mission and bring the good news of Jesus Christ to a world in need, it first must begin by teaching biblical stories for their eternal truth. Of course, good preaching is the first essential. But teaching the depth of the biblical story at every level is essential to mission. Where do we begin?

Teaching Bible Basics

While I was serving as the vicar of a mission congregation in California, I put together a Lenten series of classes designed to be offered to visitors as well as our own people. We were having a difficult time getting people to attend. I asked one man why he could not bring someone to the program, since I knew that he was a leader in his community and that he always was able to get people to do things. His answer taught me a lesson. He said, "People are afraid that they will be embarrassed by how little they know. No one wants to go to something that will make them seem uninformed, especially when it comes to the Bible. Who wants to admit they don't know the story?"

I asked others and they agreed. It was hard enough to get our own people to a Bible study, let alone guests.

This led me to ask around about how to deal with this dilemma. A Lutheran pastor named Mark Neuhaus, a good friend and brother in Christ, gave me an idea. He suggested that I go to the root of the problem and offer something that would be useful to everyone attending. He said, "Offer a Bible 101. That is, start with the basics." Mark has since passed away. I will always be thankful for his friendship and good advice.

I worked with Mark's idea and came up with what I now call "Bible Basics," a five-week course introducing people to the foundational teachings of both the Old and New Testaments. The course had to be deep enough to reveal the eternal truth of several lessons, but simple enough to be taught in everyday language. In *The Purpose Driven Church,* Rick Warren points out that Jesus taught with everyday examples we now call parables. The idea made sense.

Over the past ten years I have taught hundreds, maybe thousands of people about the basic stories of Moses, about the Psalms, about the prophetic writings, about each of the Gospel accounts of Jesus' ministry, his life, death, and resurrection, and about the church in its early days. In five weeks, with some homework, people have come away with a foundation for further study. That has always been my goal. I have never intended to make someone a biblical scholar in that short course.

Over the years I have learned how to make the material interesting and, most important, how to get some good discussions going. I have been able to adapt this to part of the confirmation process and to assist newcomers to the church.

What I advertised is what they got: learning the very basic truths of the Bible. The response was good from the beginning and it has grown over the years. The proof that my friend Mark gave me a good idea is that well over half of those who began with the basics have gone on to more detailed study. Maybe more important is that this has become an evangelism tool. I have had the pleasure of offering this to several community groups who had no church affiliation. Many people have asked about learning more. I invite them to church.

The EMC needs to bring people to Christ, but when we introduce them we had better help them understand his words. The Holy Bible is "the inspired word of God." The word *inspired* comes from the root, "in spirit." The spirit of God is revealed in its words. The Bible is God's word written. The entire Bible, not just parts of it, contains God's eternal truth. It is "written for our learning" (Romans 15:4, RSV). We are to hear God's words, and study and digest them so that they can become relevant in our lives. Anglicans teach that the Bible contains all things necessary for our salvation. To a new Christian, learning from the Bible is essential for their formation and growth in the faith.

If a relationship is going to be meaningful we must understand it. Teaching and preaching are the first phase of mission. The rest of what we do is dependent on how well people understand the message.

Coming to Jesus

Some Christians feel that a conversion moment is necessary. I don't know how many times I have been asked, especially by evangelicals, "When did you come to Jesus?" or "When were you born again?" Others ask, "When did you give your life over to Christ?" I have a problem … I don't know for sure when this happened to me.

For many of us who have spent a lifetime as Christians, we have been on a journey. The journey has taken us through several moments when we have encountered Christ and with each of these holy moments we have committed ourselves deeper and deeper into our faith.

I understand those who practice adult baptism. They hold that a conscious decision to be born of the Spirit, that is to be baptized, is necessary for eternal salvation. I agree. Somewhere along the line we must confess that Jesus is Lord. But in my tradition, Holy Baptism is a sacrament of God's grace. God makes his part of the covenant at the moment of baptism and we spend our lives keeping our part of the agreement. Becoming "Christ's own forever" is God's gift to us: our gift in return is to come to know him and love him in a lifelong journey. That is why Christian formation is so important.

No matter which journey one takes, knowing Christ is essential. One cannot confess that Jesus is Lord unless they know who he is.

A Man Who Met Jesus

The story of Nathanael's encounter with Jesus in the Gospel of John (John 1:45) is worth extra study. Nathanael was introduced to Jesus by Philip, who Jesus had just asked to follow him. It is important to note that this was an act of evangelism. Philip's friend doubted that anything good could come from Nazareth. Philip persisted. "Come and see," he said. Then, in the meeting between Philip's friend and Jesus, an epiphany took place. Nathanael confessed to Jesus, "You are the Son of God." (NRSV).

Before Nathanael could confess his faith, someone had to tell him to "come and see." The very first act in the formation of any Christian is evangelism, to call them to *come and see*. For this reason the entire process of starting the Christian journey usually begins with a "come and see" invitation.

A "Come and See" Example

A neighbor of mine introduced me to a fellow who reminds me of Nathanael. We met at a neighborhood poker game. Can anything good come from a poker game?

The guy was quiet as we played our nickel and dime game, but as the evening came to an end he asked me if I could talk to him for a minute. We stepped aside and he said, "I know you are a minister. I have some problems and I wondered if you could help." "What is the matter," I asked. He told me that he was having some troubles in his business life and that they were causing a strain on his marriage. I suggested that he get some business assistance and see a marriage counselor. He said, "I think my problem is deeper than that." I replied, "Don't neglect the practical, but maybe you should also see your priest." I knew he was Roman Catholic. He asked, "Can you be my priest?"

Since I felt it would be inappropriate for me to minister to someone I knew from our neighborhood poker game and because he already had a priest, I was hesitant to offer help. The pastor in me, however, suggested that I would think about what might help.

The next day I called a Roman Catholic priest I knew who worked with family problems. I asked if he would call my neighbor. He agreed and called him. After that, I didn't hear from either the priest or my neighbor for several months. Then one day I ran into the priest and I asked what happened. He said, "I introduced your neighbor to Jesus and I think he is doing fine." That was too easy.

What I later learned is that the priest got the man and his wife to go to a Cursillo weekend. I have experienced Cursillo myself. The word *Cursillo* is Spanish for a short course in Christianity. It is a life-changing learning experience for many. It was for my neighbor. One of the lessons from the weekend is that you are to "make a friend, be a friend, and lead a friend to Christ." My friend was taught well. His life has changed and he is doing fine making all sorts of friends for Jesus.

The EMC was there for my neighbor. It taught him about the Christian faith. It reached out and lifted him up and brought him to Christ. This is what Christian formation is all about: making people new, transforming their lives, by introducing them to our Lord and Savior.

Chapter Four Essentials:

1. Christian formation is a lifelong process of growing in faith.
2. Learning leads to understanding; understanding leads to faith.
3. In his great commission, Jesus asked us to "teach them."
4. Christian formation must be both interesting and worthwhile.

Chapter Four Question:

What are the things your congregation offers for a lifelong learning experience?

"Be present, be present, O Jesus, our great High Priest, as you were present with your disciples, and be known to us in the breaking of the bread..."
Prayer before Communion, Book of Common Prayer, page 834.

CHAPTER FIVE:
Worship in the EMC

Several years ago while visiting friends, my wife and I attended Mass at a large Roman Catholic parish in northern Indiana. As the liturgy began, the priest opened with these words, "Let us take a moment to bring ourselves into the presence of God." I was struck with the importance of what he said, and every time since, when I have presided at worship, I have begun with those same words. I have since discovered that those words, or similar ones, are used at the opening of many Roman Catholic rites. I have also learned that several other traditions use similar words. Bless them all.

If we believe in the real presence of Christ then we should say so. Jesus assured us that when two or more were gathered in his name, he would be with us. This is the most important thing for us to remember when we gather for worship: Christ is there among us.

Worship has many styles and even many meanings, but if it is truly Christian, Christ our Lord is present. With this in mind we have the responsibility of making what we do acceptable to our Lord who, in fact, is the host of the banquet we attend. The respect we must show is the reverence with which we participate, and how the joy which we are given is the blessing from being with him.

For most of the history of the church, worship has been a spectator activity. From the time of Constantine in 314 until the start of the Great Reform of the church led by Martin Luther in 1517, worship was only in the eye of the beholder. The priest didn't lead worship; he was the only one necessary at the Mass. People only watched. The Elevation of the Host, most historians say, was so that the people could see what the priest was doing. That later became symbolic as an offering to God. The bells at the altar told the people when the bread and wine were transfigured into Christ's body and blood. The words in Latin (or in Greek) were not important to the people since they were not their words, but the priest's private conversation with God, undertaken on their behalf. This was an important characteristic of the chapel church.

When Martin Luther came along, one of his leading reforms was to include the people in worship. He introduced the use of the common language and he began prayers of the people. He added hymns for the people to sing God's praises and the people were invited to receive Holy Communion, both bread and wine.

It wasn't until 1968 when Vatican II changes were put into place that the people became active in the worship experience in the Roman Catholic Church. Vatican II also brought change to most mainline Protestant churches. A liturgical renewal began, this time with the people as central to the experience.

What emerged after Vatican II was the merger of the Catholic understanding of the presence of God in the Mass to the Protestant understanding of the participation of the faithful. The two together formed what is now the mark of the EMC worship, the people praying together in the presence of God.

Prayer is essential to worship. Some contemplative people pray quietly and more charismatic people pray verbally with arms raised in praise. Either way, prayer is communication with God. It is prayer that brings us into the real presence of our Lord. In this act we open ourselves not only to address God, but to listen, as well. Hearing God's holy word is an act of prayer, as is celebrating his sacraments.

Worship and prayer have taken many forms in the history of the church, usually changing within the context of the times.

Stained glass windows, for example, were first used to tell biblical stories to the people who could not read. They were an aid to worship. They later became part of the beauty of the worship setting. Puritans who could read had no use for them, so for those wanting to purify worship, the windows were taken out of the churches. Some of us still think they're beautiful.

Like the stained glass windows of another time, today's EMC is employing new means of communication. Windows have become projected visuals, but the essential remains: we pray to the ever present God. Someday the visuals will be outdated to give way to a new medium.

Worship in the presence of the Lord, in many ways for two thousand years, has included four essentials. First, there is prayer and praise. Second, there is God's word. That is followed by confession (of faith and of sin) and finally reconciliation. These are found in many styles, but praying, singing God's praises, hearing the Scriptures and sermons about them, along with statements of confession followed by Eucharist or reconciling prayers is the usual form of Christian worship. We call this form liturgy. Liturgy has many varieties; some are ancient and some contemporary. The essential ingredient of either is that Christ is present.

For the EMC, the presence of Christ is essential to the work of the church. When we bring someone to Christ, where is it that they will meet? The encounter with our Lord can happen anywhere, but the place where we know that he is present is in worship. For this reason the EMC is strongly concerned about the quality of the worship experience. Liturgy should never be taken lightly.

Worship Is Not Entertainment

I was interviewed by a newspaper reporter several years ago when I was working with a new congregation in California. The reporter wanted to know if the worship in the new church would be contemporary or traditional. I answered that I hoped it would be holy. She thought I was trying to duck her question, so I explained. The style of worship is not as important as the content. It is what is said, not how it is said or sung, that truly matters.

I explained that what that particular congregation was going to use was becoming known as *blended worship*, that is, a traditional worship style with some contemporary music. The reporter said that would be hard to sell to a new audience. I reminded her that worship is not entertainment. What would be important, I insisted, was the quality of what was being done. She reported that traditional worship would be mixed with contemporary music; she missed the whole point about attention to quality.

Some congregations have found that particular styles, offered at particular times, are useful in attracting certain groups to worship. Their contention is that more contemporary music with a rock beat and visuals attracts younger people, while more traditional hymns and traditional settings attract older people. This works well in larger congregations where there are enough people to offer these options.

There are many exceptions to the rule. Interestingly enough, there are some blended styles that attract both young and old. In some college campus ministries, High Mass with "smells and bells" is becoming popular. At Trinity Episcopal Church in Lawrence, Kansas, they are offering a "Solemn High Mass" every Sunday evening. College students love it. One student told her parents that the "old guitar service" wasn't as meaningful to her generation. She was attracted to prayer and candles. The essential is that worship communicates the presence of God in word and sacrament.

The use of visuals is not exclusive to younger people either. Today, traditional settings seem to have broad appeal. Some congregations are finding success using traditional worship in what might be called a new medium.

When I came to St. Martin's the worship style was divided into what they called traditional and contemporary. Although our early service was always and has remained traditional for those who are comfortable with King James language (thee and thou), once a month the church had a "contemporary service." I soon discovered that there was no middle ground for this. You either were for it or against it. Some would skip church on that week. When something is that divisive it is not worth having. I ended that practice as soon as possible.

First, the service was not contemporary; it was a "Folk Mass." This included '50s music that went out of style in the '60s. It was also very loose with little order and very little focus. It was hard to differentiate this service from entertainment.

After a great deal of work with the worship committee and with Jim Wanker, our very creative music director, we shifted the emphasis to the presence of Christ. We decided that in our main 10 A.M. service, we would use some traditional hymns along with some truly contemporary music, especially in the anthems and at communion time. We also set out to explore the use of visuals in the traditional Book of Common Prayer service. The key was the presence of Christ and the attention to detail that his presence among us requires.

We discovered that the EMC in many Christian traditions has done a great deal of work in developing materials that communicate with today's media. We invested in projection equipment, including treating our walls so that they could act as screens for our visuals. I don't care for actual screens; they seem tacky. When our projection was off, the walls were just plain white. We purchased DVDs and CDs as well as some great new arrangements of some very standard hymns. What resulted was a new style of worship.

We introduced it slowly so that people could get used to the changes. You know what sudden change does to people. We used evolution not revolution. The new music was introduced almost one hymn at a time. We were willing to adjust to what didn't work. There were a few hymns that didn't get beyond their second singing. Then the words to prayers and hymns were projected on our new treated walls, and the people seemed to like what they saw. Older people were happy because the words were easy to read. We added all of the prayers and responsive readings. Finally, videos were projected along with some of the music, illustrating the words.

The result was a greater participation in worship. As their priest I noticed people looking up, rather than looking into their books. They were actually looking at one another. People didn't have to hunt for the prayers: they sang hymns, some new and some traditional, without flipping through pages to find them, and at communion there was a sense of unity. Later, prayers for healing were added and large numbers of people began to take part. Worship was alive and so were the people. As one result, attendance grew and is still growing.

After much attention to detail and focus on the presence of Christ, the mission of the church was captured in what we did in worship. We proclaimed God's word, we prayed, and we were united in Holy Communion, all in a setting befitting God's presence.

Other EMC congregations in other traditions have had similar experiences. Using the presence of God as the key and the importance of communicating his word and sacraments, we have found a way to be the place where we can bring someone to our Lord and know that the two will meet.

As a priest in the Anglican tradition I lift up the real presence of Christ in the celebration of the Eucharist. To me this is the realization of Christ's presence. In the Catholic tradition this is the Holy Mystery of the Mass, the presence of Christ in the blessed bread and wine, our Lord's body and blood. For others the Lord is present in the proclamation of his holy word. In both cases the center of worship is the presence of Christ among us. To the EMC the essential is that God is with us, and in that presence we are in communion with him and one another.

Worship Is a Time for Evangelism

What is a better time to evangelize than when we are in the presence of God? Worship should be a time when we can introduce someone to our Lord. If our worship is prayerful in a way that allows the newcomer to participate, we have an opportunity to truly introduce someone to Jesus Christ.

A growing group of mission-minded clergy is promoting the idea that worship can be an opportunity to evangelize. Baptisms, weddings, even funerals bring people into the church. Many of them are strangers and are not sure what is going on. Often the same thing happens at Christmas and Easter when people attend church with friends or out of a sense of some sort of subconscious obligation. The EMC is learning to welcome these people in new ways. Rather than throwing the book at those who are new or have been absent, some are opening the Good Book for them to hear. Sermons and prayers that tell biblical truths should be presented so that the new person might understand.

Worship must be easy to follow, it must include the newcomer, and it must celebrate, without apology, the presence of God. Worship should never be dumbed down or secularized for a special occasion. If it is worship, it should be worship. If worship is to lead someone to Christ, Christ must be invited, as well.

The most important part of evangelism is to welcome people. One of the most damaging things a church can do is to make someone feel that somehow they are either not qualified or are not good enough to take part in the worship service. This is the reason that I appreciate the denominations that welcome all baptized persons to receive Holy Communion. That says you are welcome in the presence of the Lord. We will share his presence in communion with you.

There is a movement these days in some circles of the EMC to offer what is being called "open baptism." That is offering baptism to anyone who seeks it, no questions asked. The same thing, to a lesser extent, is happening with Holy Communion, which is being called "open Communion." While I agree that these sacraments should be open to all who seek them and the welcoming church should encourage the invitation, there still is an obligation to honor these rites of the church with proper preparation and study. We may be onto a good idea in being open, but this is an area where the EMC must still do some homework. Christian formation is very much needed in the process of being open.

For those in mission, the church provides an opportunity every time it gathers in worship. It is a time when the good news of Jesus Christ is shared and it is a time when lives can be transformed into something new. In these times when large numbers of people are absent from the church, worship and evangelism are words that should go together.

If Christ is present in our worship, we have an obligation to invite others to be there, too. When they come, we have another obligation to make the introduction.

Worship Transforms Lives

A man came to worship and was made new. I will call him Charles. That's not his real name, but for his privacy and because there are many like him, we will simply call him Charles. He was truly transformed by the presence of Christ in the mission church.

Charles came into the church office one Tuesday morning asking for directions to a health center. He said he was new to the area and he had an appointment to get a physical checkup. He could not find where he was going. Since there are several such centers in the Hudson area, I asked him which one. He gave me the name of a place I didn't know, so I went to the phone book. Sure enough we found the place and I told him how to get there.

Charles seemed to want to talk some more. I was busy planning a special service, so I was trying to end our conversation.

But Charles kept on talking. I'm glad he did. It seems that he had lost his wife a few months earlier and he had moved to Hudson mostly to have a new place where he could quietly mourn his wife's death.

As we talked, I asked him if he had found a faith community since he moved. I think his real reason for asking directions at St. Martin's was to see what kind of church we were. He confessed that he was interested in finding a church and that he wondered about our church since he passed it every day. I couldn't miss the chance to invite him to worship.

I inquired, "What is your faith background?" He said, "My wife was Catholic." "What about you?" I asked. He replied, "I used to go with her once in a while, but I never joined." "Were you baptized?" I asked him. "When I was a teenager," he answered. He said that it was in another denomination. "That works for me," I said. He seemed to be relieved that his credentials were in order. What he didn't know is that I would have been just as happy if he had told me he had never set foot in a church in his life. I wasn't trying to check his ID, but rather to get to know where he was on his journey. The church should never have rules that keep people from worship.

I have had many widows and widowers come to the church. I have found that most women who become widows find it easy to come to church as they mourn. Men, on the other hand, find this much more difficult. It may be a man thing or it may be our culture. Whatever the reason, I was delighted that Charles sought out St. Martin's.

Charles joined us on Sunday and the EMC began its work. The presence of Christ became real for Charles. The first thing he said to me after worship was that he enjoyed the service. We had just begun to use our projected visuals for the hymns and for the prayers. Prayer books are troublesome to newcomers. User-friendly worship is one of the most important things a mission church can offer a new person. Charles was part of the worship on his first visit. I could tell worship moved Charles; I could see it in the smile on his face.

Then he told me how much he liked the music. When I came to St. Martin's I had told our music director that what we should do is enter the church in reverence and leave it in joy. Our creative music minister knew exactly how to do that. Charles experienced uplifting music on his first visit, as well.

But the EMC did its best work at the coffee hour. To me the reception after the formal liturgy is an important part of worship. We enjoy the fellowship of those with whom we have just shared communion.

Several people approached Charles and introduced themselves. Charles told his personal story to one man who quickly introduced him to another widower. Within a few weeks Charles became involved at St. Martin's. His life was changed. In the Lord's presence Charles was transformed and so were we. He came to know Jesus as he never knew him before. Charles became active in a variety of ministries and he became part of the fabric that is the EMC.

Stories like his are common in parishes like St. Martin's. The reason for the existence of the EMC is to welcome people wherever they are in their faith journey. Some are seeking God's peace, others need fellowship, some are not sure what they want to find, but they know something is missing in their life. Whatever the situation, the mission church opens its doors and people like Charles find that our Lord is present to make them new.

Of the two churches Charles could have found, I'm glad he walked into a mission and not a chapel. I think he would agree.

Chapter Five Essentials:

1. Christ is present when we gather in his name. Worship should honor his presence.
2. Worship is how we communicate with God; prayer and his holy word, as well as the celebration of his sacraments, are communication with the present Christ.
3. Worship should be so user-friendly that one can participate on their first visit.
4. Worship in the EMC can change lives.

Chapter Five Question:

Is your worship fitting for the present Christ? Do you make it easy for a visitor to meet him?

"If your enemy is hungry, give him bread to eat, if he is thirsty, give him water to drink." Proverbs 25:21, RSV

CHAPTER SIX:
EMC, Ministers to the World

The past several presidents of the United States have all called upon faith-based organizations to help when the nation has found itself in need. They have always responded. Churches in mission and ministry in times of need are part of the American experience. From the time of the American Revolution, to this very day, churches always have been a shelter from the storm when they are needed. Ministry to others in the world is part of the Christian fabric.

After September 11, 2001, President George Bush called on all faith-based organizations to help heal the people of New York. My own denomination sent people from all over the nation and opened several of its churches near Ground Zero as rescue missions. St. Paul's Church located near the World Trade Center was spared. It served as a place of service and prayer for most of two years following the attack. A plaque in thanksgiving for service to the community is now displayed there.

While churches in New York opened their doors, places of worship in all parts of the nation opened their doors, as well. Churches from coast to coast were packed on September 11 and for the days following. Mission and ministry are part of what it means to be a Christian in times of crisis and even in ordinary times.

Where It All Began

St. Paul wrote instructions on ministry to the Ephesians as those first-century people learned what it meant to do the work of the body of Christ (Eph.4). Paul told them:

There is one body and one Spirit, just as you are called to the one hope of your calling, one Lord, one baptism, one God and Father of all, who is above all and through all and in all. But, each of us is given grace according to the measure of Christ's gift. (Eph.4:4-7, NRSV)

He went on to say that each gift is part of the one body to which we have been called to serve. Each of us, Paul taught, in our own way, are to minister "to build up the Body of Christ until all of us come to the unity of the faith."

Think about the importance of what Paul taught. A ragtag group of faithful people, gathered together mostly in secret, were called to be the Body of the Risen Christ in the work they had to do. How impossible; this had to be a God thing.

They persevered and together became the foundation of the holy catholic church, which today has nearly two billion believers in every corner of the earth. On their own they might have served themselves and a few neighbors, but as the Body of Christ with gifts from God they helped change the world. This ministry could only happen with God's grace and the power of the Holy Spirit. Yes, one Spirit, one God and Father of us all gave Paul's friends what is our model to follow. The church is all of us, with our many gifts, acting together as our Lord's hands and feet, and arms and legs serving here on earth.

One Man's Encounter with Ministry

One Sunday morning a man named Robert ran into an old fraternity brother named Sam while coming out of his suburban Chicago church. The two had been close friends at the University of Illinois. They shared a warm greeting and a few memories. They agreed to have lunch during the following week.

Sam was visiting Chicago on business from Cleveland, where he lived. Robert lived in the Chicago suburb of Arlington Heights, where he had been employed as a marketing executive for a large company. Robert had lost his job just a few weeks prior to the meeting with his friend. They met for lunch at a small deli-style place in the suburb. Robert didn't know how to tell his classmate that he was out of work. He was embarrassed, so the conversation began with the sharing of pictures of their families.

Then Robert swallowed hard and said, "Sam, I'm not doing too well. I lost my job and I have no idea what I will be doing. My savings will not last forever and I need to work. Do you have any ideas?" Sam wasn't sure if Robert was fishing for a job or just looking for someone to talk to, but he knew his friend well enough to talk it out. "What do you want to do?" Sam asked. Robert replied, "I just want to be worth something to the world. I know I have skills that are valuable to some company out there, but I don't know where." Sam paused for a moment and asked, "Have you talked to your pastor?"

There was a silence. The two had met in church so it was a reasonable question. Robert had never thought of speaking to his pastor about his job. "No, I haven't," said Robert. His friend asserted, "I think you should. I know he can help you get through this tough time." Well, Robert took the advice and things began to change.

Robert soon discovered that his church had begun a program through its men's ministry to support men dealing with a variety of business challenges. He had an encounter with the EMC in action. Robert became active in the program. First he was introduced to a prayer group of men who had been through similar difficulties. They prayed together once a week and included each other in their personal daily prayers. He had become very aware of the power of prayer while his children had been dealing with serious illness. Robert's entire family prayed together throughout their struggle and emerged healed not only in body, but also in mind and spirit. Prayer had become natural to Robert and now it was so very timely.

The group not only lifted its members up in prayer, but they ministered in a practical manner. They had formed a network of businessmen who were seeking employment with companies seeking people. They also sought ways to get people retrained with new, more marketable skills. The group, which had become an ecumenical movement, was becoming known for its positive action. Over the years they had many names: Christian Business Leaders, Businessmen in Action, later, as women joined the ranks, Business People in Action, and much later, The Between Jobs Ministry. Nationally there has been a countless number of similar business support groups formed.

In the early 1980s when Robert found himself in need, this type of ministry was new. He stayed with it long after he found work, and later he became a leader in what he felt was a special calling. Since then, many forms of this ministry have begun in a variety of places. Today mission-minded churches of all denominations reach out regularly to people in economic need. Not just the homeless, not just the poor, but to people of all walks of life who find themselves in need of the same combination of prayer and action, as Robert needed in the 1980s. As for Robert, he has done well. He went on to a fine new job and has since retired to become a neighbor of mine in Florida.

In the economic downturn of 2008-2009, it is the EMC that is offering a wide variety of career ministries designed to aid the unemployed with prayer and practical help. In a May 20, 2009 report, the *Tampa Tribune* offered an article on the mission church's role in helping people in difficult economic times. Tribune reporter Michelle Bearden wrote, "Congregations across the religious spectrum are responding with free support groups that provide prayer and practical advice such as how to reinvent yourself and the art of navigating Web sites to find career opportunities." The report noted that dozens of Tampa Bay area churches began these ministries while similar programs were being started by congregations in cities across the nation.

This is the EMC in action, Christ's body in motion.

Ministry Means Service

Jesus gave his disciples an example to follow. "I am among you as one who serves," he told them (Luke 22:27, NRSV). The word minister comes from a Latin word that means servant. Likewise, the word deacon comes from the Greek word which means servant. To minister is to serve.

For those of us ordained in the catholic tradition, we are first ordained as a deacon before we become priests. There is a movement to change this. I personally hope this does not change because it is important for all clergy to first be a servant. Of course, others who are ordained as "ministers" by definition are servants, as well. One who is a pastor serves his flock.

Bishop Gethin Hughes, my friend and bishop for many years, always stressed that those of us who worked in his office were servants of the people of our diocese. He was a servant bishop and we were to act accordingly. For that reason he had us answer our telephone, "The Office of the Bishop, serving the Diocese of San Diego."

Being a servant is what it means to be a minister. Whatever ministry one might have, lay or ordained, by definition it is as a servant. The EMC is not as concerned by the ranking of clergy as it is about the ministry of the laity. For most of the EMC these days, there is a call that begins at baptism which speaks of the priesthood of all believers and the ministry of all baptized people.

Serving Includes Those Served

I had an opportunity to visit another pastor at a neighboring congregation one day. We were going to be working on a community project together, so we planned a meeting to go over the details. When I walked into his office I noticed a sign on his desk which read, "Give a person a fish and you feed him or her for a day, teach a person to fish and you feed them for life." I noticed the sign right away because I have the same well-known saying folded in my wallet. We began our conversation about that little bit of wisdom.

My friend told me what it meant to him. I made note of what he said. He commented that besides stressing the importance of teaching, it also spoke of the fact that the minister has an obligation to get the person receiving outreach involved in the process. He said, "What good is it if we only give things away and we never ask them to participate? People can't always be the recipient. If we are to be the church in mission we must bring them into what we are doing. Who better to reach out to someone else than a person who has received themselves?" I have my friend's comments tucked away in my wallet right under the teach-a-person-to-fish saying.

Both the OCC and the EMC have many fine ministries. My friend and I agreed that the difference between the two is that the chapel is in a giving mode and the mission is in the involving mode. Chapels are the ones giving people a fish and missions are teaching people to fish.

Too often these days we look at our ministry as what we are giving to others. Yes, that is important, but what are we doing to lead them to be part of the Body of Christ? The church in mission is not about giving things away just so we feel good about ourselves. One man told me he thought the church's outreach was how much we gave away to the poor. I told him there is a whole lot more, like bringing someone to Christ. I don't think he understood.

Many wonderful people give things away; bless them, but they are not the church.

Giving things away is a good thing and there are many secular and civic groups that do that very well. I am proud to say that I have been a Rotarian for many years. "Service Above Self" is our motto, which means something special to each of us in the organization. Our motto states that we are to put others before ourselves and we are expected to give of our time, talent, and treasure to that end. We do that quite well.

But Rotary and the other fine service organizations are not the church. They help others in very meaningful ways and they make the world a better place, but unlike the church this help ends with assistance. In the church is where we should be beginning. When we have helped a person deal with a physical problem, we should then remember their mind and spirit. When we have served these things in one way or another, we should then remember the salvation of their soul.

In our secular world it is not politically correct to speak of one's eternal salvation. But we are not the secular world. The church has become very secularized. I even hear people say "Happy Holidays" in church when they should be saying "Merry Christmas."

We are the universal church which has been called to be in mission and ministry. We are to go out into the world helping others, but then we are called to make disciples of all nations, teaching what Jesus taught and baptizing in the name of the Holy Trinity. If we go out into the world in ministry we must include in our "service" the invitation to know Christ.

When Jesus ministered to the woman at the well, he spoke of living water. He taught the woman that the water of the world is needed to quench our thirst as we live our daily lives, but the living water (which is understood as baptism) is for our eternal soul. In the same way our ministry sometimes provides water for today, but water for the soul is the fullness of our mission.

Congregations find their spirit in their mission and ministry. "Activity cures anxiety," a woman once told me. When we are busy serving others we are not dwelling on ourselves. When we are doing things for others in the name of the Lord, we are letting our light shine as Jesus taught in Matthew's Gospel. "Let your light shine before others so that others may see our good works and give glory to our Father in Heaven" (Matt. 5:14, NRSV).

The health of a congregation and the validity of its ministry are directly dependent on what happens in mission and ministry. The future of the universal church depends on each of us using our gifts. When the light shines in service, others will see and come to know our Father in heaven. If the people St. Paul taught about their gifts had not used them in harmony with each other, the Christian faith might still be limited to a few cities in the Mediterranean. Instead, the light of Christ has shown the way to people everywhere. Lord, let the light keep shining.

Chapter Six Essentials:

1. We offer our particular gifts in ministry to be part of the Body of Christ. Each in our own way, in this union, we become the whole church.
2. Ministry in the EMC changes lives.
3. Ministry must include help for the soul.
4. The EMC lets its light shine so that others might see, and give glory to our Father in heaven.

Chapter Six Question:

What ministries are offered by your congregation to invite people out in the world to be healed in body, mind and spirit?

"He said to them, 'Come and see,'" John 1:39, NRSV

CHAPTER SEVEN:
The E-word, Evangelism in the EMC

The Gospel of John gives us this: "Andrew, Simon Peter's brother, went and found his brother and said to him, 'We have found the Messiah.' He brought Simon Peter to Jesus …" (John 1:40-42, NRSV). This was the first recorded act of Christian evangelism.

Jesus later sent his followers out to tell the good news of the Kingdom of God. Our Lord instructed them: "Proclaim the Kingdom of God …" (Luke 9:2, NRSV) and "Go therefore and make disciples of all nations …" (Matt.28:19 NRSV). In other words, go out in the world and be my messenger. That is evangelism. The word comes from the root word, *angel* which means messenger.

Evangelism transformed a man I knew.

A convert to the Christian faith that I knew in California once asked me why someone hadn't told him about the good news of Jesus Christ earlier in his life. He became a Christian after moving to California from Korea at age seventy-five. My answer to him was that I wished we had met earlier in his life, but I thanked God that someone led him to Christ and that we became friends when we did. He died at age eighty, a very happy brother in Christ.

What brought this man to Christ was evangelism. I wish someone would have led him to our Lord sooner, but I am thankful that the power of the Holy Spirit transformed this man when someone asked him to "come and see."

He told me that several men in the Korean community where he lived were Christian. When he moved to his new community he didn't speak a word of English, but he discovered that his neighbors were learning it. They were taking classes at the local Korean Presbyterian Church. He was invited to join them. At that church he was introduced to Jesus Christ. He told me, in English, by the way, that his life was completely changed. He was no longer afraid of his new country because he knew he was loved by brothers and sisters in his newfound faith.

This man, at the end of his earthly life, found a completeness that not only gave him God's love, but made him into a light for others to see. In a way his newfound peace in Christ became an example for other Koreans. In fact, he became an evangelist himself. He led dozens of his friends to the faith that they could see changed his life. The gift of the Holy Spirit came to this man in time for his life to be complete; it was not too late. The evangelism in an EMC that brought him to Christ is a sign of the living God. The Holy Spirit that he came to know, by his example came to those he knew: that is evangelism.

Evangelism: The Life of the Church

The Holy Spirit is the breath of the living church, the Body of Christ. The essential sign of life to anybody is breath; evangelism is that sign in the life of the EMC. Without the breath of evangelism the church would die.

As important as evangelism is to the life of the church, we tiptoe around the subject, hoping that no one will ask us to be part of it. The problem for most of us in the Christian faith today is that we are either too shy or afraid to go out and be a messenger for the Kingdom of God. One fellow in my congregation put it this way: "You can ask me to do anything here at church. I'll sweep the floors and wash the windows. I will serve on any committee and I will do lots of heavy lifting, but don't ask me to be an evangelist."

This good man was at least honest and he meant what he said; he did all sorts of thing around the church. What he didn't know is that he was already an evangelist. He was telling people the good news just through his actions.

One of St. Francis of Assisi's most famous sayings is, "Always preach the Gospel, and when necessary use words." All that we do in the name of Christ is our testimony, our sometimes unspoken word, that Jesus is Lord. When we act in a Christ like manner, we are proclaiming the Kingdom of God, when we serve others in Christ's name we are sharing the good news, and when we let our light shine as Jesus taught, we are truly evangelists.

Many of us picture an evangelist as someone standing on the street corner asking, "Brother have you been saved?" I guess that person might be called an evangelist, although I would argue that he or she is not really being a messenger for the good news of the Kingdom of God. Where is the good news?

Evangelism, in the biblical sense, is to bring someone to Christ by word or deed. Conversion is up to God. "Come and see," as Phillip said to his friend Nathanael (John 1:46, NRSV). The invitation is something that we must offer, but the transformation of the spirit is the Lord's work.

All that we need to do as Christians is to encourage others to "come and see." For that reason I contend that all Christian ministries should have an element of evangelism. The lay leaders of all of the congregations I have served, I'm sure, were tired of hearing me say that all of what we were called to do in the name of Christ should be considered evangelism.

In this section of this book we have looked at Christian formation, worship, and ministry. All of these should be functions of evangelism in the EMC. In the mission church when we reach out to love and serve our neighbors, we do it with the good news of Christ as our motivation. This means we are evangelists. In the chapel church, the motivation may very well be doing something good, but it is not always intended to lead someone to Christ.

In the EMC, by our calling in the great commission, evangelism comes first, it continues, and it concludes in all we are called to do as disciples. We lead a person to Christ as we teach them, as we worship with them, as we minister to and later with them, and then as we send them out to be examples for others to see. That is the evangelism cycle, inspired by the Holy Spirit, so that the process can start all over again. The evangelist is the light holder, so that others may find their way on the journey to becoming an evangelist themselves.

Without evangelism the apostolic church would have ended about the year 80. We are not sure what year the last apostle died, but sometime around the year 80 or 85, about a half century after the resurrection. If none of the twelve, and those who shared ministry with them, had not been evangelists, the Christian church would have died when they did. But the Holy Spirit was given to them and they became the one holy catholic and apostolic church.

Instead of just being a group of twelve ordinary men, as they were, they became extraordinary. They were so empowered by the Holy Spirit that they began a movement to reach all corners of the world. The historic apostolic faith has been handed from generation to generation to this very day by evangelists. There are now two billion of us. All of this started with evangelism from twelve everyday ordinary men, not much different than most of us. Evangelists like them for two thousand years have kept the faith, shared the faith, and then passed it on.

In the OCC, people lived in places where the church was part of the culture. For most of the history of the church, the faith was passed from parent to child within the loving confines of the chapel.

The problem for us today is that the culture in most places in not necessarily Christian. We don't have the comfort of a chapel that we share with our children and grandchildren. Sometimes I wish we did. In order to pass the faith on to the next generations, we have to do as the early church did; we have to ask people to "come and see."

A Great Evangelist

The fellow I mentioned a few pages ago, who said he would do anything but evangelism, is not alone. That is the attitude of many in the church today. One woman I met while visiting a church in Hamilton, Ontario, Canada, could be described this same way. She told me when I visited that she was the quiet type. She did things behind the scenes and was quite content to just be one of the people in the pews. "I will do whatever work our vicar asks, except evangelism," she told me.

What I later learned about this dear woman was that she took food to shut-ins; she baked pies for people when they were ill, and she led the prayer chain in her congregation. Everyone knew her. One person after another at that lively church told me that she was one of the reasons that they found their way to that church. This is the woman who would do any work but evangelism.

What the EMC needs are more people like this "non-evangelist." Maybe we need to change the word. If the word evangelist is misunderstood so much that people are afraid of it, maybe we should come up with a new word. I've thought of using the word missionary, but I have been told that word gets a bad rap, as well. How about "light holder"? People who are such good examples of the love of Christ that their light shines so that others might find their way. The lady in Canada was surely a light holder. I think we need a better word, but you get the idea.

I'm still looking for a good descriptive word to use in place of evangelism. The word may not be as important as the action. The EMC must be the church going out into the world as messengers of the good news of Jesus Christ, but as of this writing that is still called evangelism.

Evangelism is not about numbers; it is about mission.

I have been asked by many congregations to lead programs about congregational development. I enjoy this work because

I see the honest desire by so many people to build up the Body of Christ.

One question I usually ask is, "What is the most important thing your congregation needs to do right away?" The answer usually is, "We need new members." This reply tells me a lot. First, this means that they understand church growth as something they can control with some sort of special effort, and second, they feel that new people are needed so that their congregation will survive. The problem is that they are wrong on both counts.

As Rick Warren pointed out in his book, *The Purpose Driven Church,* "Only God makes the church grow." (p.14) What we are called to do, Warren says, is plant the seeds, nurture what we have planted, and God will do the rest. Second, if we think that we need new people to survive, we have missed the boat about what it means to be in mission. The people struggling with life out in the godless world are the ones in need. They need the loving kindness of our Lord. We have something they need to "come and see." The church in mission is not about us, it is about those who have yet to join us.

What happens when a congregation shifts from survival to mission is that God's abundance begins to provide all that they need. There is an old expression: "Love is not love until you give it away." This is the abundance of God. It is what I call God math. It defies logic. The more love you give away, the more love there is. The same is true with all of God's grace. Faith and hope, just as love, are abundantly ours. These are the assets of the mission church. What they offer as dividends are the gifts to missions usually revealed to us in growing numbers of people. Study after study in church development show that congregations grow in size at the same rate as their missions grow. This is God's abundance providing for the mission, not an effort to get enough people to continue our chapels.

The lights we shine in the EMC always lead others to see. If our ministries are truly using God's abundant love, the "come and see" element is natural. People naturally want to be part of something that is active and full of life.

The excitement of mission is another of God's abundant gifts. As one lady put it, "I feel the joy of Christ when I help out at the shelter." She was speaking of a women's homeless shelter in Florida. Knowing how difficult the work is in that place, I know it must be a God thing for her to feel joy. That is how God leads us in evangelism. As difficult as it is, it is a joy.

St. Francis, in his wonderful prayer, teaches us, "It is in giving that we receive." Jesus taught us that "it is more blessed to give than to receive." What we give in mission we receive back over and over again. Each time we do something to lead someone to the love of Christ, we also are being led to the joy that God grants us for our gift. This is more of "God math." Evangelism is a gift we in the EMC are called to give and from it we receive joy … abundantly.

Chapter Seven Essentials:

1. Evangelism comes from the same root word as messenger; to be an evangelist is to be a messenger of the good news of Jesus Christ.
2. In the EMC we let our light shine so that others will come to know Christ.
3. Evangelism is not for us, but for those we bring to Christ.
4. Lives are changed when people come to our Lord.

Chapter Seven Question:

What is your congregation doing to lead others to Christ? Do you call this evangelism?

PART THREE:
The Journey from the OCC to the EMC

"Pray to God, but also row for shore." Russian proverb

CHAPTER EIGHT:
Measuring Our Course

A woman who was serving on her parish evangelism committee attended a communications workshop I conducted many years ago entitled Building Better Congregations. She asked me how her congregation might, as she put it, "get some evangelism." I told her that evangelism is not something that we could get by going over to Kmart. She laughed at what I said, but I could tell I didn't address her question. In my presentation I noted that evangelism is a form of communication. It tells the gospels' stories through both word and action. I tried to explain that evangelism should be included in all we do in our ministries. I could tell she still didn't understand, so I said, "See me at the break."

She came over as we took a few minutes for cup of coffee. Her question was honest. She wanted to know how her congregation could get started on doing the thing that I had just told her was essential to the success of their ministry. We talked for a minute, but I realized that I had some work to do. I had to find a way for this woman to measure a course for the journey that she wanted for her congregation.

This conversation got me started on a study of congregational development. I have been at it for more than a dozen years and the work is not complete. It may never be. I am still seeking ways to map the journey for this woman, so that congregations like hers may become the EMC.

Taking the Journey

I hope that reading the pages of this book so far have convinced you that the world needs the EMC. And I hope that there is a desire to move toward that calling. The OCC has served its purpose and now God is calling upon the church to be in mission by moving bit by bit toward the EMC.

Let the journey begin. There is an old saying that you will never get anywhere unless you know where you are going. God will lead us in any journey we take, but we must listen and observe to know where he wants us to go. We will also have to take the steps of the journey. The destination is God's; the journey is ours.

The trip from the OCC to the EMC is not something we can find on MapQuest. That is the problem. Our journey to the mission church may be destined for some back roads and detours. The complexities of our contemporary society and the challenges of the secular world may make our journey a winding road. No one has ever said that the road to the EMC will be a simple trip. But I believe this will be a road well traveled if we have the courage to start the journey.

To find our way to becoming the mission church we must first determine:

- Where we are in our congregational life: What is our history?
- Where we are in our faith: Are we consumers of faith or advocates?
- Where we are in our ministry: Are we disciples?
- Where we are in our desire to answer God's call: Are we missionaries?

Standard Congregational Measurements

There are a variety of ways to measure the starting place of a congregation. This is not a geographical map. It isn't the Twilight

Zone either. It is someplace on the faith road: where we are in our history, where are we in our faith, and where we are in our ministry.

My congregational development professor, Arlin Rothauge, developed a measurement of congregations nearly thirty years ago that has been a standard since. He used membership to define congregations.

- Congregations of up to 50 members were called <u>family churches.</u>
- Those having 50 to150 members were called <u>pastoral churches.</u>
- Those having 150 to 350 were <u>program churches.</u>
- Those with more than 350 were considered <u>corporate churches</u>.

Dr. Rothauge outlined his observations of the ways these churches behave. The family church was lay-driven with close ties among members; the pastoral church was very dependent on the minister; the program church was driven by its ministries with less dependence on individuals; and the corporate church usually had a large staff with many programs.

These descriptions still hold their value although the numbers may have changed. It has been my observation that each of these categories should be increased by about fifty now, or should reflect average Sunday attendance. The reason for the change is the aging of most mainline congregations. Without younger members, more people are needed to do ministry. Attendance reflects participation. The dynamics, however, have remained the same with the exception of a few congregations which have retained the style of their past. One corporate church I know still behaves the way it did when it was pastoral, leaving the pastor worn out.

Family and pastoral churches are usually the OCC because that is their nature given their size and ability to do ministry.

Program and corporate churches are usually growing and by their nature they are the EMC.

Another measurement of congregations is more qualitative than quantitative. It was offered in a book by Carl S. Dudley and Sally A. Johnson titled, *Energizing the Congregations* (Westminster Press, 1993). Dudley and Johnson measured congregations not by size, but by what they call their images. Churches are divided into these images: Survivor, Prophet, Pillar, Pilgrim, and Servant. Each image represents a style of ministry and a definition of purpose. The numbers of members do not determine the image. Some congregations have more than one of these qualities.

The Images

Survivor: congregations dedicated to their own survival.
Prophet: congregations with a prophetic mission such as
        social justice.
Pillar: congregations of community leaders.
Pilgrim: congregations that have gone out on a mission,
sometimes "daughter" churches.
Servant: congregations dedicated to serving others.

Most OCC churches today would be called survivors. Churches which were born with a prophetic mission might be EMC or might be OCC depending on whether the focus is Christ-centered. Pillar churches are the congregations of community leaders. They have great potential to do good work. They often are the social "in" place and can be either OCC or EMC depending on how they conduct their ministry. Pilgrim and servant congregations both have a purpose, and if that purpose is Christ-centered they are the EMC.

Neither of these measurements, quantitative or qualitative, if they are taken for their face value, will offer us a place on the map in their journey. History along with these descriptions will give us something to measure. Rothauge offered what he called the *life cycle* of congregations. He suggested that when a congregation is born it has energy to do its work; as it matures it falls into a stability which is a comfort zone, which leads to its decline and eventual death. This is an OCC model.

Rothauge offers a remedy for the declining cycle which he calls *parallel development*. This is the development of new ministries during the life cycle. These new ministries will replace the old and begin new cycles of their own.

The Rev. Charles Fulton III of Start Up, Start Over suggests that the hope is in the resurrection of a congregation. He says that the life cycle in resurrection goes from death to rebirth, meaning that death of the old way leads to birth of the new way. These concepts, of course, are in line with the EMC.

The measurement for a congregation includes a little of each of the above. The size of a congregation is best defined by its place in the life cycle. Many mega-churches started with a few dozen members. Many once large churches now stand empty; remember my trip to London. The images of the churches are only important to the focus of what they are doing. If they are Christ-centered and not self-centered, any of these images can be the EMC.

My friend Canon Michael Durning, assistant to the bishop in the Episcopal Diocese of Southwest Florida, has reminded me that what is most important is average Sunday attendance (ASA). Canon Durning likes to measure ASA over several years when he works with a congregation. He says that attendance, not membership, indicates the status of a congregation. He says, "Congregations seeing an increase in ASA are doing something right." True enough. The Diocese of Southwest Florida must be doing things right because its ASA is three times the national average.

For those seeking to move from OCC to EMC there are three things to determine. These three will triangulate their position and give them a starting point for their journey.

- First, is ASA consistently increasing?
- Second, is the mission of the congregation reaching beyond its own doors with meaningful Christ-centered programs?
- Finally, is the congregation, in its mission, inviting others to know Christ?

If all three of these can be answered yes, the congregation is already the EMC. Whichever questions are answered no require steps yet to be taken on the road to the EMC.

ASA and Mission Questions to Ask

If attendance is increasing, is it due to the increase in population? The same question might be asked about a decrease. If our growth is from our mission activity and not just the added population of our town, we are closer to our destination. For this reason it is important to consider population growth when we place ourselves on the map toward the EMC. Some congregations grow at only a fraction of the population growth. In fact, they are losing ground.

Is our mission considering the demographics of our area? Just as we consider population growth, we must also consider demographic changes to our population. One church I know actually opened a child care center in a retirement community. The mission and ministry of the EMC must reach out to the reality of the community in which it lives. If this is on target, the congregation is closer on the map to the EMC.

These questions may be answered by research gathered by an organization called Percept. The Percept concept is to use demographic data of an area to determine where on the development map a congregation falls. They profile a wide variety of information, including things like income levels, education, religious preferences, worship style preferences, and even things like community involvement. Percept developed a program in the late

'90s to identify the demographics of a community using standard marketing and census research and then to identify the demographics of a congregation using the same measurements. The difference was called the "gap." The journey would be to close the gap from where a congregation was to what Percept referred to as "where it ought to be." Using this highly reliable data, a congregation may not only learn about their community, but also learn about itself. In this process, a direction for ministry will be on course.

When a congregation has identified the reality of its community and the reality of itself, it has found its place on the map for the journey toward the EMC. It is then time to make a plan of action or a "to do list."

A "To Do List" for the Journey

- A mission plan must be designed employing the essentials in this book.
- It must be organized with clear assignments and timelines for those on the journey.
- There must be motivation for the travelers, things like recognition of tasks that are well done, plus enthusiasm (which attracts) and sincerity (which convinces).
- There must be an empowerment of the travelers. They will be empowered by the Holy Spirit, but they also must be empowered though the leadership of pastors and lay leaders to reach their destination.
- Finally, the travelers must be willing to adjust to conditions. They must be willing to retake part of the journey when conditions change.

Most congregations have seen a glimpse of the Promised Land when they have observed other congregations which have already made the journey. It is helpful to see what those other congregations have done on their way. Observing what has worked for others is always useful.

Every congregation must look at itself as a group of pioneers heading out into the wilderness. It must be willing to take risks, trying new things and discovering what works and what doesn't. Remember the people of God who followed Moses? They struggled in the wilderness, but the Lord provided for their journey and the Promised Land was theirs. In much the same way a new promised land is waiting for us, as well.

Some of the church is old and tired.

Data from my own denomination is often depressing. Like many mainline denominations, the Episcopal Church is in decline and its congregations are mostly OCC. There are some wonderful exceptions and I celebrate them. I was blessed to be the pastor of a great EMC. I also have served in dioceses with many great EMC congregations. But the denomination as a whole is suffering. The Episcopal Church's *2008 Faith Communities Today Survey* shows that fifty-three percent of the parishes and missions were founded before 1901, most are in what are now poor locations with buildings seating less than two hundred, and the ASA of more than half of the congregations is below seventy. The net loss from deaths, adjusted by baptisms, is 19,000 people a year. Another 20,000 are leaving the church for other reasons which I would call a lack of mission or the loss of faith. The decline nationally is nearly five percent a year.

What concerns me most is that there is little direction for these old tired congregations. Most of them are left to find their own solutions. The Episcopal Church has done very little to help the parish church; in fact, some of the programs have led to decline.

Preoccupation with secular issues and politics has dominated Episcopal national conventions and little is being done by church bishops to refocus the mission of the church. The church is in denial. I don't believe church leaders aren't concerned; I believe mission is just not their priority.

For the most part, declining congregations come from the OCC era. Time has passed them by and they have been left out in the wilderness to die. Most of these churches are aging so fast that they will be gone in another ten years.

These old churches will have completed their journey if something is not done soon. For some, a Christian burial would be a kind thing. For others there is always the hope of resurrection. Some OCCs seeking to become mission-minded are finding support, usually on their own initiative. Some have taken advantage of programs for congregational development available from many ecumenical sources. The effort has come from the grass roots, not from headquarters.

In some places, new birth is needed. Some mission-minded denominations have answered the call for new churches. They have placed top priority for new church "plants," that is, the starting of new congregations. Most mainline denominations, like my own, are not among them. The advent of nondenominational churches is very interesting. Most of these new congregations are not independent churches, but rather are members of evangelical associations. They use the term nondenominational almost as a marketing tool because many people are tired of the old mainline churches. Charismatic leaders often start these congregations. Those churches holding that person in very high esteem often close when the leader leaves. A few have already found themselves on the declining side of the congregational life cycle. Often this happens when their original mission is lost to complacency. However, Christ-centered nondenominational congregations that gather in Christian fellowship and reach out in their communities have proven to be successful.

Meanwhile, old churches are declining and closing. Some OCC churches have abandoned the faith for secular causes. Others have tried to keep the faith in denominations that have given up on their vision. An ecumenical office in California reports that declines exist in all mainline Protestant denominations and in the Roman Catholic Church. Old congregations just can't make it as they were. The Roman Catholic Archdiocese of New York has closed thirty-five churches over the past ten years. They are not alone.

Hope Is Eternal

Where is the hope? The hope, of course, is in the Lord. Pope Benedict XVI wrote in his book, *Saved in Hope*, "Faith is the substance of hope." (p.30) He wrote that our hope comes from our faith in the Risen Christ acting in our lives.

Through our faith the church will survive; that is our hope. But it will be different. Most of us in the church have heard the famous last words: "We have never done it that way before." There is always resistance to change. People find it difficult to give up what has been their comfort zone sometimes, thinking that warm and fuzzy place is somehow holy. Of course, it is not. But in the journey toward mission, change is essential. Our changes should not be undertaken just to be different, but rather they should be a revision of our efforts to meet the current reality of our world. If we are to lead others to Christ in today's environment, we must minister in this environment.

God will lead his church to do what it needs to do, but for many of us the road will end where we are currently standing. God in his mercy will still love those who are left behind in the OCC. But God is calling others to do his work. Someone else will take up the journey for us, if we don't go down a new road to the place God wants his church to be. One day there will no longer be that little old church down the street and there may not even be an Episcopal Church, but God's universal church will survive, simply because it is his.

For those of us who answer the call, there is an exciting road ahead. That is part of our hope. This road is one of new adventure, one where we will be doing exciting new things and discovering the joy of being in the EMC.

One Congregation's Bold Journey

Several years ago I attended a congregational development conference given by Percept in Santa Fe, New Mexico. At the meeting there were pastors from several mainline denominations, all seeking answers to the question of how the church will survive. Mike Regele, an ordained Presbyterian minister and the founder of Percept, led the presentation. He stressed the mission of the church and the hope that is given to it in the power of the Resurrection. He asked each of us to share our experiences as we broke into our discussion groups.

I met a group of very fine pastors. One was a Lutheran from a large Midwestern city. He shared his very moving story. I will not use his name or the name of his congregation, both for his privacy and because his story could be the story of many who have moved from the OCC to the EMC.

This man was the pastor of a church that one year earlier had less than eighty members. In its heyday the church was home to more than eight hundred. What remained were a few old members who still lived in the old German neighborhood. A few others, out of old friendships, traveled back to the old neighborhood from the suburbs. ASA was less than fifty. The youngest person in the parish was sixty-seven years old. The average age was seventy-eight. By this pastor's calculation the congregation would be gone in less than five years. This was a good example of the OCC.

One year before our conference this man decided to face reality. He went to his synod office and suggested that the church should close and the property be sold with the money going to support another ministry. He would retire.

A group of mission-minded pastors came to visit and see the situation for themselves. They discovered an old, tired group of faithful people who just didn't know what to do. They also discovered that the community demographics were dramatically changing near this church.

Two of the visitors and the local pastor went out for a cup of coffee. As they sat in the coffee shop listening to several of the young people gathered, they realized how the community had changed. The area was fast becoming home to college students from the university located a few miles away. They were buying or renting old homes in the area and converting them to mini-dorms and fraternity houses.

Jokingly one of the men suggested that the church be converted into a Starbucks. Sometimes mission ideas come direct from the Holy Spirit. The three men laughed and then fell silent. Could that be an idea? Why not turn the church's parish hall into a coffee shop for college students? They got started. After long discussions and detailed planning, a coffee shop was opened complete with computer outlets and reading material. It had nice tables and good lighting and it was made welcoming with attractive signage and displays. Coffee prices were very reasonable. It was designed to be a Christian outreach ministry for the community. Some of the old church members were finding new energy serving coffee to college students. One woman said, "It reminds me of when I was a student."

Within in a few weeks the shop was paying for itself and it became a gathering place for discussions and fellowship. Within a few months a weekly Bible discussion group began to meet at the shop, which led to the founding of a Christian Fellowship of Students. A Sunday "brunch" service was launched at the shop and within one year a new congregation had formed at this old church. ASA at the "brunch" was more than one hundred and growing. This old tired place was born again; an OCC had become an EMC. Talk of closing the parish was gone. They were too busy doing God's work.

This congregation located themselves in the reality of their community and reached out, bringing the light of Christ to a new generation of people. They made the journey to the EMC.

Chapter Eight Essentials:

1. Congregations are defined by size, image, and history.
2. Each congregation has a life cycle.
3. Study attendance trends and the reality of ministries.
4. Prepare a "to do list" to move toward the EMC.

Chapter Eight Question:

Where is your congregation now, and where is it headed?

"All things are possible to one who believes."
Mark 9:23, NRSV

CHAPTER NINE:
Motivating the EMC

Ralph Waldo Emerson once wrote, "Nothing great has ever been achieved without enthusiasm." The EMC proves Emerson right. One common denominator for this new mission church is enthusiasm. The word enthusiasm comes from the root, "in God or *en Theo*." What the EMC does is *in God*. The excitement I have observed in the EMC can only be described as a God thing. This is why so many of us find these mission-minded churches so refreshing at a time when so much of the church is still stuck in the old chapel.

There is an old expression that enthusiasm persuades and sincerity convinces. The truth of this is that without enthusiasm the process of convincing cannot begin. It takes enthusiasm to motivate someone to their conviction.

The Greatest Motivation

In the liturgy of many denominations comes something called the "comfortable words." They are a series of reassuring passages form Scriptures. I am particularly fond of the words from John's Gospel that most of us know by heart:

> *God so loved the world that he gave his only begotten Son to the end that all who believe in him will not perish, but have everlasting* life (John 3:16, RSV).

These very comfortable words are the greatest motivator of the church. Comfort, knowing that my belief in Jesus Christ means my eternal salvation, is all the motivation I need to keep my faith. It is also all the motivation I need to lead others to Christ. These words make it clear that there is no greater reason to lead someone to Christ than the eternal salvation of their soul.

If we are to set our course for the journey we discussed in Chapter Eight, we now need to remind ourselves why we are doing what we are doing. We as the church in mission are called to know Christ and to make him known. Our ministry was given to us in the great commission (Matt. 28:16) to make disciples of all nations. The motivation for what we are called to do is to know that the gift we might give someone is awesome. It will mean that they also may believe as we do and find eternal life.

The Motivation at Pentecost

Fifty days after the Resurrection the faithful were gathered in Jerusalem for the feast of Pentecost. At this event the universal church was born. It was given the power of the Holy Spirit and the first noticeable result was that people could understand one another. Understanding, and the unity from it, was the first motivation given by the Holy Spirit for the church to enter into its mission. From that moment, described by Luke in the Book of Acts, the church was motivated to go to all parts of the world.

The same Holy Spirit is calling us to understanding and unity to move from the OCC to the EMC. In our own times there is a new call for mission. The comforter, the Holy Spirit which Jesus promised will help us, is creating an inspiration among many to go into mission. The word *inspiration* comes from the root, "in spirit." The energy we feel when we go into mission, like the joy we feel in doing God's work, comes from the same source that motivated that crowd in Jerusalem two thousand years ago.

The Holy Spirit has motivated the church throughout its history. Great leaders of the church have been inspired to do great things. St. Paul was moved to take the church to the gentiles, not a popular notion to many. Pope Gregory the Great was led to reorganize the church in his own time. Over the centuries the Holy Spirit motivated St. Francis, Thomas Aquinas, Martin Luther, and Queen Elizabeth I (with her great Anglican compromise). In more recent times, C.S. Lewis, Henri Nouwen, Billy Graham, Martin Luther King, Jr., Mother Teresa, Desmond Tutu, John Paul II, and a host of others have all been moved by the Holy Spirit to add new life to the church.

Now it is our turn. We are called to become the EMC. But you may be saying, most of us are not these great people of history. True, most of us will not go down in history as some of these people have, but the same Holy Spirit will motivate us, just as it motivated them. For most of us, our contribution to the mission of the church will be a corporate act. That is, we will join with our brothers and sisters as the Body of Christ to do the work God has given us.

We will exercise our inspiration in the unity that was given at Pentecost. St. Paul used that power when he took the church to places far and wide in the Roman Empire. His skill at organizing and motivation can be found in his letters to the congregations he founded. What he offered his flock was encouragement and a well-outlined discipline to follow. He gave them hope and direction. We should study his teaching. His results were unbelievable.

St. Paul taught the early church that the Holy Spirit would guide them and give them the energy they needed to do God's will. What will motivate the OCC to become the EMC comes from the same energy. Like Paul's followers, we need a clear focus for our purpose. For this discipline is needed.

Bring Order Back to the Church.

Several years ago a wonderful lady, who was a parishioner at the time, asked me to define discipline. I wasn't sure why she wanted to know such a thing, so I asked in what context she was asking. She said that her grandchildren were wonderful, but they were not very well-behaved. She was concerned that they were not learning what is acceptable and what is not. This is an issue of our times.

I gave her a simple answer about discipline. First, I told her that discipline was a word that had fallen upon bad times. To many the word has become politically incorrect. Dr. Spock and the permissiveness of his writings, taught back in the '60s, had given the word a connotation of repressiveness, when, in fact, discipline is freeing. Second, I reminded her that in the Bible we see many teachings about learning to follow the law and about being responsible for our actions. These, I told her, are about discipline.

Learning is what discipline is about. Learning to do what is right and learning how to act in a responsible way is what discipline teaches. Discipline is being in control to do what is right. This is something we must all learn. I think that is what my parishioner needed to hear.

All of us, children and adults, must learn to exercise discipline or we will fall into chaos. Jesus taught us to pray, "Lead us not into temptation, but deliver us from evil." If this is our prayer, it should also be our action. Exercising self-discipline is the responsibility of every Christian.

All of this reminds me that as Christians we are called to various disciplines.

First, our basic moral behavior is the discipline of keeping God's law. The Ten Commandments are the foundation of this. Then there are the teachings of Jesus, who came not to replace the law, but to fulfill it.

Second, there is the discipline of being a Christian: loving God and our neighbor as well as having faith in Jesus Christ. This discipline means we have a responsibility to live out the vows made at our baptism, and for those of us who are ordained, the vows we made. For married persons it is to live out those vows, and to all, it is the discipline to live our lives in thanksgiving for Christ our risen Lord.

Finally, there is the discipline of being a disciple. The word disciple comes from the same root word as discipline. That means being willing to do what God calls us to do. This may be the most difficult discipline of all. The first two disciplines only require obedience to the basics. The discipline of being a disciple requires us to give ourselves up to God; it is a discipline of *sacrifice*, another word that has fallen onto hard times.

So here we are wondering what is happening to the church these days. We are seeking to move toward being the EMC. Yet we have problems with two words that are required for our discipleship: *discipline* and *sacrifice*. Neither word these days would do well in a recruitment brochure for membership in the church. Yet, both are asked of one who commits themselves to a life following Jesus Christ as their Lord and Savior.

In all traditions discipline has fallen upon hard times. Some denominations have moved so far away from discipline that there are no rules at all. Like the child without boundaries, people wonder aimlessly without any guidance. They find themselves trying to figure what is right and what is wrong without any standards to follow.

The Methodist Example

The United Methodist Church has, as one of its long traditions, a document called *The Book of Discipline*. The book is updated from time to time, but it has served as the outline of order and discipline of the denomination since the beginning of the Methodist movement. Most say it has served them well.

In this book there are detailed listings of things that individuals and congregations are called to do as part of the discipline of the church. The notion of personal sacrifice is found here. There are lists of social principles one must follow. These are instructions for how one is to behave as a church member and there are explicit things that individuals, congregations, regional districts, and conferences must do. The book goes into great detail on the functions of committees and the missions of various ministries.

I think other Christian denominations would do well to read these pages. It offers a concept that could be very valuable to many in the journey toward the EMC. It is a focused outline of what is expected of a member of the church. The bits of Methodist polity are not important. What is important is the discipline and sacrifice to follow Christ in the mission of the church.

A Motivated Bunch of Good Christians

I remember the old television program *Mission: Impossible* that ran long before the series of movies with the same name. What I liked was seeing the adventure of something that was supposed to be impossible. Each week the characters would get an assignment and each week they would overcome obstacles to do what seemingly could not be done.

Maybe it is the adventurer in me, but I love that kind of challenge. If someone says it can't be done, I want the job. I know where this came from. I had a teacher in high school who always told his students that we could do whatever we set our minds on. "Nothing is impossible to one who believes," he told us. I didn't know back then that he was quoting Mark 9:23. Nevertheless, it stuck. I have always believed that if we have faith, and if we understand where we are going, we can get there.

Several years ago I was discussing my confidence in this concept with two friends from church. That evening we agreed that nothing is ever accomplished without a belief in what one is doing and faith in God that somehow it will be accomplished. We shared ideas about being "can do" people and we quoted Luke's Gospel (1:37, NRSV), "For nothing will be impossible with God." We decided to call our conversation, "Possibility Theology." Nothing much ever came of our idea except that one of the fellows in that group went on to invent a medical procedure for heart surgery, another built a successful large business from an idea he started in his garage, and the other entered the ministry after twenty years in business. The latter is also author of this book.

What we all knew is that God calls us to do things and we must listen. We also knew that if the inspiration lingers and isn't some passing fancy, we better look into it. It is God who is calling. If the Holy Spirit is persisting and our "mission impossible" is waiting, we better answer. Of course, if God is asking us to do something, it *is* possible.

God is asking the church to bring the good news of Jesus Christ to people of our times. Congregations are being called to begin what might seem impossible. Fear not, the reality is that it is an exciting adventure with God at our side. The mission toward the EMC is not impossible. As each of us participates in this godly enterprise we must remember that with God all things are possible.

Chapter Nine Essentials:

1. The promise of eternal life through our belief in Jesus Christ is the great motivator.
2. The Holy Spirit will enable us to do what we are called to do.
3. We must focus with faith, discipline, and purpose to what God is calling us to do.
4. Our task may seem impossible, but with God all things are possible.

Chapter Nine Question:

What is God calling your congregation to do and how are you answering the call?

"Let everything that has breathe praise the Lord, Hallelujah!" Psalm 150:6, NSRV

CHAPTER TEN:
Celebrating the EMC

The journey is not over when you reach the Promised Land. It wasn't for the ancient Hebrews and it isn't for us. That is where the new journey begins. When we finally become an EMC, that's when we get started all over again.

I remember working with a congregation that spent nearly three years building a new sanctuary. It was a long journey and the people of this congregation were indeed proud to have completed the difficult work to get everything done on time for the beautiful dedication service. The new church was magnificent. It truly was an accomplishment to the glory of God.

I met with the building project team after the dedication for a final debriefing of the project. As we finished our meeting there seemed to be a collective exhale from all of us. But we knew that we were now going to have to put this beautiful facility to use. The pastor of this congregation thanked all of those who had served on the committee for their fine and sometimes difficult work, but he called on them for new work. Each person was asked to celebrate the new building with a new ministry. He passed out a list of things that they might choose form. It was called the "celebration list." The pastor said, "Prayerfully consider which celebration you feel called to do. This is your thanksgiving for where God has led us."

I have always thought that the word *celebration* is underused in the Christian faith. We celebrate the sacraments and we celebrate other rites of the church, but we should also celebrate the work of our ministries. The word means to "proclaim, to honor or to perform publicly that which is solemn." The ministry which we are called to do as the EMC is to be celebrated.

When we have arrived at the place in our journey that our congregation can be considered an EMC, let the celebration begin. We are not just celebrating the completion of a journey, but we should be celebrating the beginning of one. Like the congregation with the new sanctuary, we also have something new to proclaim, to honor, and to publicly perform. Like the celebration of a new marriage or a new ministry, the celebration of an EMC is to enter into a new relationship with one another and with God.

God calls us from the OCC to be transformed into the EMC and God calls us to transform others as we have been transformed. This is a celebration.

The Celebration of God's Call

The relationship with God our Father has matured over the course of human history. From the fall from grace of the first human beings, our creator has been calling us back to his loving arms. The changes God has granted us have come exactly when we have needed them. This is his plan that we should come to know him better and better. It is the celebration of the glory of God.

God created us out of love and he has cared for us in the same way. Each time he has given us something new it has allowed us to know him better. This again is the celebration of the glory of God.

I find it interesting that the changes we have been given all come through inspired actions from God. Moses was inspired to lead his people, the prophets were inspired to call the people back to God, and in the fullness of God's inspiration he sent us his only begotten Son for our salvation. These are another celebration of the glory of God.

As an old-style communicator, I also find it very interesting that the inspired technology of our times have given God the mediums to communicate and celebrate with us. Like the inspiration of Moses and of St. Paul, every inspiration we may have, God may use for our benefit.

When communications were passed from one to another by chisel and stone, we received the Ten Commandments etched in stone for eternal endurance. When paper and ink were invented, St. Paul was able to circulate his messages to the church in mission. When the printing press enabled the world to read, the church was reformed, so that people could read in their own language. Now we have electronic communications. Like each of the previous inspirations, God is using this gift as a celebration that we will be able to get to know him better.

Paul's inspiration set forth the mission, the first EMC. Then came the chapel where prayer and contemplation carried the faith forward. When the printed word came along, God used the reform of the church so that we could get to know him better. This celebration was a return to the EMC. Today new technology is given to us so that we can, again, get to know God better. Today, technology allows us to communicate in ways never known before. God wants us to celebrate this tool so we can know him better and, in turn, we can share his holy word with others. This is a celebration for the EMC.

What Will Our Celebration Look Like?

First of all, our celebration is our action to proclaim, to honor, or to perform publicly that which is solemn. Second, it is to the glory of God and not to us. Finally, it is the beginning not the conclusion.

But what will it be like? We can never see the future exactly as we might like, since God may have things planned for us that we cannot imagine. I love the bumper sticker that reads: "Want to make God laugh? Make plans." The celebration of our ministry as the EMC will be new and different. There is no way we can make a list of things that will distinguish the EMC of the future. All we know for sure is that change is certain. Yet, we have confidence in knowing that God's eternal truth is our never-changing foundation. We will have to celebrate knowing that the great adventure that God has planned for us will take us to a place where he wants us to be. For that we should all rejoice.

There are a few things we can say about the new EMC. We know that it will be new and different. We know that it will be filled with opportunities for us to love and serve the Lord, and most important, it will be what God wants it to be. The EMC is where the church is called to be. It is the church flexible enough to do God's will when God calls us to do it.

The two churches of this essay are both part of the Body of Christ. But the OCC has already served its purpose and the new EMC is being called to pick up the torch to be the light of Christ in a new generation. This is our celebration.

A Congregation in Celebration

A 2002 ecumenical pastor's group meeting in Chicago shared this true story.

A church in a Midwestern suburban community found its way through several years and types of transformation. It went from being a new mission to an established chapel, and then declined. But in a renewal of its spirit, it was born again to become a great EMC.

This congregation was founded as what Dudley and Johnson call a "pilgrim" church. It was a mission of a large urban congregation sent out to a new growing area back in the '60s. Its task was to bring the faith to people who moved into the area. At first it was successful. The little mission congregation formed with the intention of being a church for many who were moving "out to the suburbs."

As the population grew, so did the church. With financial support from the "mother" church, it built its first building and then another. Within a few years there was a sanctuary seating three hundred, a parish hall, an education building, and an administration building. The five-acre campus was the home to more than six hundred parishioners. The church did well for several years through the ministry of several skilled pastors. Then decline began to set in.

One very popular pastor left the church under unpleasant circumstances. This was followed by a group of people leaving because of a disagreement over church finances. Additionally, the church became split over the styles of worship. At its low point there were fewer than one hundred members and ASA was forty-five.

These classic congregational problems escalated other problems. It was as if one thing led to another and the very existence of this once thriving congregation was in peril. The final blow was the resignation of the treasurer, who informed the church board that the church was "broke."

This once thriving congregation was always the OCC. It never was able to focus its ministry toward the context of its community. For this reason when local population growth leveled off, so did church growth. Decline began when the church found itself in a comfort zone unaware of the changes in the community.

Several parishioners went to the denomination's district office seeking help. The plan of action designed by the district and a parish committee was to try to keep the church open. First, a loan was granted from the district to pay the church's bills. Second, an emergency board was set up to determine its financial future, and finally, a group of mission-minded pastors gathered to examine the ministry of the congregation. The most important of these was the work of the pastors.

What this group of five found is that the decline came when the people took their focus off of their mission and put it on themselves. The solution was to renew the mission and refocus the purpose to the realities of the time and place.

The community had changed from its original demographics. What were once dream houses for people moving out of the city were now starter houses for young couples. What was once a community of people who were loyal to their denomination was now a place where the vast majority of the people were unchurched. What was once an up-and-coming area to live and raise a family was now a temporary place for very mobile people.

When the pastors examined the reality of the community they recommended a shift in ministry. The new reality required mission work that the old congregation never knew. A missionary team was brought in to help refocus the work of the church. The team was charged with the responsibility of setting a plan for evangelism, the creation of new ministries, and the development of worship that would engage new people. The old congregation balked, but they had no choice. They were forced to go along with the changes.

Fortunately the missionary team had good pastoral skills. They made their first priority to be a teaching mission for those already in the parish. They then identified good leaders to be the new local missionaries. Through a process of teaching and step-by-step revision of the style of ministries, the missionary team was able to transform the congregation into a future EMC. New ministries were launched. A new pastor was called to help lead the new mission.

Even before the church became an EMC people began to come to worship. There was a renewal going on and it was obvious. There were a few "gatekeepers" from the old church who tried to keep changes from happening, but the momentum was too great. A new day had come and it was not to be denied.

The celebration of this renewed congregation actually began with the first steps of the missionary team. The energy from the Holy Spirit could not be mistaken. People were attracted to this church. The congregation was transformed and so were the individuals involved. This was a celebration.

However, the great celebration began when the new leadership began leading people to mission and ministry. The congregation had made a complete shift from OCC to EMC. ASA was back up to two hundred and growing. New ministries were attracting people and new people were getting involved.

The new work led this church into outreach ministries for young couples and single parents. It included a child day care center and a babysitting ministry that would give working couples and single parents a night out. The church hired an experienced child care provider to run the center, but an agreement was made so that faith-based materials could be used and religious instruction was available. The parents' night out was made available by a group of parish "grandmas" to any couple or single parent who attended the church more than once.

Other new ministries were developed to meet needs in the community. A business lunch group was formed for local business people. They were given a place to gather in Christian fellowship. Home prayer groups were formed to help introduce people to the church. A women's ministry was started to help working mothers share faith experiences with their children. A similar program later followed for dads. Care was taken to see that each of the new ministries provided an opportunity for evangelism. The principle was to care for people and to make the faith available to them, as well.

This is celebration at its best. This congregation was transformed into the EMC. People's lives have been and will be changed. The love of Christ has come among the people. For that we must celebrate: "Let everything that has breath praise the Lord, Hallelujah!" (Psalm 150:6, RSV).

Chapter Ten Essentials:

1. The celebration of the EMC begins with the start of the journey, but does not end when a congregation becomes an EMC; that's when it starts all over again.
2. Celebration means to proclaim, to honor, or to perform publicly that which is solemn. The EMC qualifies for celebration.
3. Celebration is to the glory of God, and not to us.
4. The celebration continues as we do the work of the EMC, changing lives and winning souls for Christ.

Chapter Ten Question:

How does your congregation celebrate its work in the EMC?

Canon William Dopp and Bishop Ernest Shalita together in Florida.

The Marion Burk Inspirational Walk at St. Martin's in Hudson, Florida.

The National Cathedral in Kampala, Uganda where Archbishop Janani Luwum was murdered in the court yard at the hands of government troops while Bishop Shalita was inside the building.

The large crowd gathered at St. Andrew's Cathedral in Kisoro, Uganda for a special celebration of the Year 2000.

Procession of more than 150 clergy from the diocesan offices down the road to the cathedral for the Year 2000 celebration.

The grave marker at the National Cathedral for James Hannington, the first bishop of Eastern Africa. He was killed by King Kabaka's troops in 1885. He is one of the many Martyrs of Uganda.

The burnt cross from the ashes of St. John's Church in Chula Vista, California. The cross is now displayed in the new church building as a symbol of the Resurrection

BIBLIOGRAPHY AND SUGGESTED READINGS

The Book of Common Prayer (Episcopal). New York: Church Publishing Incorporated, 1979.

The Book of Discipline of the United Methodist Church. Nashville, TN: The United Methodist Publishing House, 1980.

Dudley, Carl S., and Johnson, Sally A. *Energizing the Congregation: Images That Shape Your Church's Ministry.,* Louisville, KY: Westminster/John Knox Press, 1993.

Lutheran Book of Worship. Minneapolis: Augsburg Publishing, 1978.

Nicolosi, Gary G. June 4, 2000. "Mutual Ministry: A Strategy for Thriving in the Parish," *The Living Church.*

Beazley, Hamilton, and Payne, Claude E. *Reclaiming the Great Commission.* San Francisco: Jossey-Bass, 2000.

Regele, Mike. *The Death of the Church,* Grand Rapids, MI: Zondervan Publishing House, 1995.

Tutu, Desmond. *Believe.* Boulder, CO: Blue Mountain Press, 2007.

Warren, Rick. *The Purpose Driven Church*. Grand Rapids, MI: Zondervan Publishing House, 1995.

Benedict XVI. *Saved in Hope*. San Francisco: Ignatius Press, 2008.

Biblical Translations:
RSV, Revised Standard Version
NRSV, New Revised Standard Version

DATA SOURCES

2008 Pew Forum on Religion and Public Life Survey

2008 Episcopal, Faith Communities Today Survey

2008 Ecumenical Survey of U.S. Congregations

2008 Ecumenical Study of U.S. Congregational Laity

2007 Episcopal Church Parochial Reports

2009 AOL News Poll, Religious Affiliation

ABOUT THE BOOK

In 2000, Episcopal priest William Dopp and his wife Janet were on their way to Kisoro, Uganda, to be part of a special celebration at St. Andrew's Cathedral in that remote part of East Africa. On their way they stayed over in London where they had the opportunity to attend Sunday worship at St. John the Baptist Church in the Kensington section of London. The contrast between the two churches inspired this book. The old gothic church in London was nearly empty on Sunday morning. One week later, the Dopps took part in worship in rural Kisoro where the 1,200-seat cathedral was not large enough to hold the crowd. The church in London had on its literature: "Preserving Holy Worship." The church in Kisoro, Uganda, proclaimed on a sign: "Jesus is our living hope." One church lives in the past; the other is in mission proclaiming the good news of Jesus Christ. These two churches are the symbols of what Dopp calls the old chapel church, the OCC, and the emerging missionary church, the EMC. Congregations of all denominations fall into one of these two categories. Through engaging ministry experiences backed up by current statistics, Dopp illustrates how the emerging missionary church transforms the lives of people. In these lively pages he boldly proclaims that the emerging missionary church is the future of the Christian faith. He calls congregations of all traditions into action. He asks them to be part of an exciting future where the church is being called to bring the good news of Jesus Christ to a world desperately in need of God's peace.

ABOUT THE AUTHOR

In his ministry, The Rev. Canon Dr. William Floyd Dopp has served congregations in California and Florida. He has always served with deep faith and an emphasis on congregational development. Since entering the ministry after a career in communications, Dopp has had a dedication to the great commandment, to love God and one another, and to the great commission, to take the church to all people. This dedication has led to success in each of his undertakings. For six years he served as a leader in church development and as the assistant to the bishop of the Episcopal Diocese of San Diego. During that time he led a program to develop emerging congregations and build new churches. He did this while earning his doctorate in congregational development at Seabury-Western Theological Seminary in Evanston, Illinois. He holds a B.S. degree in business and journalism from Indiana University and a Master of Divinity from the Claremont School of Theology. Since retiring from parish ministry, he is devoting his time to consultation for the development of congregations in the United States and Canada. He lectures and is a regular editorial contributor to several faith-based publications. He and his wife Janet travel and split their home time between Florida and California. They have two grown sons who are both married, and they have three grandchildren.